The Theatre in Ulster

Also by Sam Hanna Bell

The Theatre in Ulster

*A survey of the dramatic movement in Ulster
from 1902 until the present day*

Sam Hanna Bell

GILL AND MACMILLAN

First published in 1972

Gill and Macmillan Ltd
2 Belvedere Place
Dublin 1
and in London through association with the
Macmillan
Group of Publishing Companies

7171 0569 5

Jacket designed by Cor Klaasen

Grateful acknowledgement is made to the
Arts Council of Northern Ireland
for financial assistance in the publication of this book

Printing history 10   9   8   7   6   5   4   3   2   1

Printed and bound in the Republic of Ireland
by the Book Printing Division of
Smurfit Print and Packaging Limited, Dublin

Contents

DEDICATED IN GRATITUDE
TO THE GENERATIONS OF ULSTER ACTORS
AND ACTRESSES WHO, FOR SO MANY YEARS,
HAVE INSTRUCTED AND DELIGHTED US

Preface

This is an account of the theatre in twentieth-century Ulster. We can find records, of course, of theatrical entertainments among us much earlier than that. Jonathan Swift's strolling players cry

> Gallants, this Thursday night will be our last,
> Then without fail we pack up for Belfast.

In 1657, William Edmunson, the Quaker preacher, fell foul of just such a tribe in the market-place of Derry; in 1785, Mrs McTier, that indefatigable letter-writer, was informing her brother that the impression made by Mrs Siddons in *The Unhappy Marriage* so overwhelmed Belfast society that 'five ladies were taken out fainting in the last act, and hardly a man could stand it'; more than a century later the playgoers of Belfast were flocking to the Theatre Royal to pay homage to Madame Sarah Bernhardt and Mrs Patrick Campbell. And about that year, 1905, the curtain rises on our story of a theatre organised, acted and produced solely by Ulster men and women.

There have been one or two studies of the Ulster dramatic movement. The best-known, Dr Margaret McHenry's *The Ulster Theatre in Ireland*, was published as far back as 1931. Since then, apart from David Kennedy's essay in the symposium, *The Arts in Ulster* (Harrap 1951), and a few magazine or newspaper articles, there has been nothing written on the development (or retrogression) of the movement. I am all the more indebted therefore to those people who searched their files and their memories to assist in the writing of this book, particularly to two notable men, both of whom are now dead: Mr Sam Waddell (Rutherford Mayne) who allowed me to examine his cuttings books dealing with the productions and personalities of the Ulster Literary Theatre, and Bulmer Hobson, one of the founders, who kindly answered my questions on the origins of the U.L.T. I hope I have fulfilled his injunction to record why that Theatre came into existence.

My thanks are also due to my friend and ex-colleague James R. Mageean, now living in San Diego, California, who untiringly answered my queries and sent me the relevant sections from his valuable collection of theatre programmes; to Mr John O'Leary, S.C., Dublin, to Mr John Moss (John F. Tyrone) and Miss Joan Keenan of the Ulster Group Theatre, to Mr and Mrs Hubert Wilmot of the Arts Theatre and to Mrs Mary O'Malley of the Lyric Players Theatre.

I am indebted also to Mr Jack McQuoid, Mr Joseph Tomelty, Mr Harry S. Gibson, Mr Harold Goldblatt, Mr Wolsey Gracey, Mr John McBride, Mrs W. R. Gordon, Mrs Maeve Clements, Sister Assumpta Saunders, Mrs Thomas Carnduff and Mr Edward Fearon, who lent me or drew to my attention material which was helpful in writing this book. I wish to thank the Lyric Players Theatre and Mr John Hewitt for permission to include his poem, and Mr Brian Friel for permission to reproduce the extract from *Philadelphia, Here I Come!* published by Faber and Faber. I am also grateful to Faber and Faber for their permission to quote from Forrest Reid's *Private Road*, to Putnam for the passage from Lady Gregory's *Journals*, to Macmillan, publishers of *The Irish Theatre* edited by Lennox Robinson, to George Allen and Unwin for the extract from *Friends and Relations* by St John Ervine, to Constable, publishers of *The Irish Drama* by A. E. Malone, to

Methuen, publishers of C. E. Montague's *Dramatic Values*, and to Nelson, publishers of *Irish Literature and Drama* by Stephen Gwynn. Where I have quoted from critical comment and from published plays I have endeavoured to acknowledge the source.

Over the years there have been a number of radio programmes on the Ulster theatre movement. These I found useful. I am grateful to Mr David Kennedy and to Mr John Boyd, each of whom contributed to this series; to the theatre personalities who took part in them; and to the B.B.C. for permission to quote from these scripts.

Finally, I wish to thank the Arts Council of Northern Ireland for the opportunity to write this short history of the theatre in Ulster. Most of the opinions and all the omissions therein should be laid to my charge.

Belfast, May 1971   SAM HANNA BELL

I

The Ulster Literary Theatre

(i) THE FOUNDING FATHERS

One evening in the autumn of 1902, two young men were
travelling homeward on the Belfast-bound train from Dublin.
They had just parted from the most remarkable group of men
and women in that Ireland of the new century and had achieved
more than partial success in the errand that had taken them to
the capital. But idealists are inclined to chafe under anything
less than complete success. Young Mr Bulmer Hobson and
young Mr David Parkhill from Belfast were, above all else,
idealists. It is not recorded at what point on that historic
journey Hobson struck the arm of his seat and exclaimed
'Damn Yeats, we'll write our own plays!' What can be said is
that that blow laid the foundation of the Ulster Literary
Theatre.

Bulmer Hobson recalls the objective and events of that visit
to Dublin.

Parkhill and I wanted to get into touch with the National
Theatre Society[1] which had been started by Maud Gonne's
Daughters of Eireann. The Fays were the producers and
Yeats, A.E., and all the writing crowd were actively helping.

They put on plays in small halls and had a little hall for rehearsals in Camden Street. Their best actors were Dudley Digges and Maire Quin. Maire had the use of Maud Gonne's house in Rathgar, A.E. was a couple of doors away. Maire invited David and me to stay with her and she and Dudley took us down to Camden Street where we met the whole crowd—Yeats, A.E., Cousins, the Fays, Seumas O'Sullivan, Fred Ryan, O'Neill, Russell and a lot more. We wanted permission to put on some of their plays and help from some of their actors. Everybody was most cordial and helpful except Yeats—haughty and aloof . . . we wanted to put on in Belfast Yeats' *Cathleen Ni Houlihan* and Cousins's *The Racing Lug*. Dudley Digges and Maire Quin promised to come and act in our first production. But Yeats refused permission. When Maire reported this to Maud Gonne, Maud said 'Don't mind Willie. He wrote that play for me and gave it to me. It is mine and you can put it on whenever you want to.' So we put on *Cathleen Ni Houlihan* and *The Racing Lug* with Dudley Digges and Maire Quin as our leading actors. Annoyed by Yeats we decided to write our own plays—and we did.[2]

But, pleasant as their excursion had been, the two young Ulstermen had not undertaken it, nor suffered Yeats' antipathy towards all things Ulster, for the sole purpose of starting a dramatic society. In a dialogue contributed by Yeats to A.E.'s weekly *The Irish Statesman*, one of the characters says: 'I generally dislike the people of Ulster, and want to keep them out.' When Hobson and Parkhill stated the full reason behind their mission the poet's coldness is understandable. It was, in short, to bring the Ulster people *in*. 'Parkhill, W. McDonald and I', says Bulmer Hobson in the letter quoted above, 'were running a small group trying to spread the ideas and principles of Wolfe Tone and the United Irishmen and met with little noticeable success. So we decided to try the drama as a vehicle of propaganda'. That 'little group' was the Protestant National Association. Bulmer Hobson has said it 'had neither a long nor an important existence, but the men whom it brought together started the Ulster Literary Theatre.'[3]

Nevertheless, in 1902 Hobson, Parkhill and their friends first named their company the Ulster Branch of the Irish Literary Theatre. Dudley Digges and Maire Quin kept their promise and in November 1902 appeared in *Cathleen Ni Houlihan* and *The Racing Lug* at St Mary's Minor Hall, Belfast. Years later, Gerald Macnamara wrote an account of that first performance:

> The Ulster branch of the Irish Literary Theatre made its first bow to the public in a small hall in Belfast. Small and all as this hall was it was much too large for the audience who patronised them on those two evenings. On the morning of the first performance the members were carrying some old second-hand scenery up the stairs to the hall when they were stopped by the caretaker who ordered them to take it away. 'This hall,' said he, 'is used for a Sunday school, and we'll have none of your damned scenery here.' As there was no time to discuss the matter with the manager of the school, the young enthusiasts were obliged to hire curtains to drape the hall in lieu of scenery. The effect of these curtains was so novel at that time that the audience applauded the set as the curtain rose.[4]

The next recorded performances were early in 1904, probably in March, when the Theatre again staged *Cathleen Ni Houlihan* along with A.E.'s *Deirdre*. On both occasions the audiences were sparse and the receipts poor. The Ulster playgoers, if they existed, seemed to want different fare. 'The Belfast public', says Macnamara, 'were not taken by *Cathleen Ni*

Houlihan. Ninety-nine per cent of the population had never heard of the lady—and cared less; in fact someone in the audience said that the show was going "rightly" till *she* came on'.

In their subsequent history the Ulster players were to find friends and support in Dublin. But at this point there seems to have been a marked lack of understanding between the National Theatre and the emerging company in the North. George Roberts, the Dublin secretary, wrote to David Parkhill informing him that the Belfast actors had no authority to state that they were a branch of the Irish National Literary Theatre. At the same time he demanded royalties from the impoverished company. There is no contemporary evidence of any money being paid, but on the occasion of the visit of the 'Ulster Players' to the Scala Theatre, London, in 1923, a brief report on the Theatre's history in the *Morning Post* of 5 July states that 'each member had to stump up to the tune of £2 10s. to pay off the debt'. On the other issue the Ulstermen's answer was simple and direct. They renamed their company the Ulster Literary Theatre and applied themselves to the task of writing their own plays.

This was in 1904. In November they published the first issue of a literary review, *Ulad*. 'Its working capital,' says Bulmer Hobson, 'consisted of £5, subscribed by David Parkhill, J. W. Good, John Campbell, W. B. Reynolds and myself, and we were the committee in charge, with Reynolds as editor and Campbell as manager.' James Winder Good, a journalist on the staff of the *Northern Whig*, contributed to *Ulad* the most perceptive criticism written on the early productions of the Ulster Literary Theatre. Later he was to assist A.E. to edit the *Irish Statesman*. The poet Joseph Campbell designed the cover of the journal, signing himself Seosamh MacCathmhaóil.

W. B. Reynolds, who was music critic of the *Belfast Evening Telegraph*, seems to have performed admirably one of the functions of an editor of a new journal—the pursuit of contributors. He invited Forrest Reid to call upon him. The novelist described their meeting:

I liked him from the beginning. He told me of the Ulster Renaissance; he told me of the new quarterly that had been started; he gave me a copy of the first number, and he asked me to write something for the second. He had already received poems from A.E. and Padraic Colum; plays from Joseph Campbell, Parkhill, and Bulmer Hobson; he had been promised articles by Stephen Gwynn and Roger Casement ... Reynolds was eloquent, optimistic and extremely enthusiastic: I felt ignorant, bewildered, and very much out of it. Although Irish, I had never been interested in politics, had never distinguished in my mind north from south, and the Ulster propaganda did not particularly appeal to me. It was not what to-day would be called Ulster propaganda, since it was definitely nationalist, and merely insisted that Ulster should play its part in the Irish Revival. I had no objection to that naturally, but I could not see why there should be two camps, nor why what Reynolds called 'the Ulster genius' should necessarily be, as he said it was, satiric. If it came to that, it was the first time I had heard of 'the Ulster genius', and I had certainly seen no sign of it. Therefore I listened to Reynolds without conviction. I didn't know what 'Ulad' meant; I didn't know why Joseph Campbell should call himself Seosamh MacCathmhaóil. It seemed to me a most difficult name to pronounce, and since Reynolds got over that by pronouncing it Joe, the difficulty still remains. I asked him what he would like me to write, and received a sudden clue as to the real bent of his interests when he replied without a moment's hesitation, 'an essay on *The Future of Irish Opera*'.[5]

2

Forrest Reid, in fact, contributed an article on the Lane Collection, then on exhibition in Dublin, and a short story, *Pan's Pupil*, the only piece of fiction to appear in the short-lived journal.

Contributors to *Ulad*, unlikely at that time to have had immediate contact with the Belfast group, were Padraic Colum, James Connolly, Alice Milligan, Roger Casement, A.E., and Stephen Gwynn. But its pages were largely filled by the young writers, artists and poets gathered under the aegis of the U.L.T.; Bulmer Hobson, Joseph and John Campbell, Francis Joseph Bigger, Robert Lynd, Carl Hardebeck, George and Norman Morrow, Edwyn Kirkby and Lewis Purcell (David Parkhill). In Reynold's editorial in the first or Samhain number of *Ulad* we find a statement of the Theatre's aims. Setting aside the editorial 'we' it is unlikely that Reynolds drafted his column without consulting Hobson, Purcell, Good and John Campbell. The emphasis on the 'Ulster' quality at this early stage is therefore interesting. The editorial begins:

> *Ulad* means Ulster. It is still often necessary to state as much; we intend to insist. This Ulster has its own way of things, which may be taken as the great contrast to the Munster way of things, still keeping on Irish land.
>
> Cities like Londonderry and Belfast have drawn all its best energies towards them. And though of late years the city has been more a stumbling-block to the right intellectual and artistic progress of the country, yet, in spite of influences and disabilities operating against it, a certain characteristic temperamental and mental trend has been lent to the town by the country, and a certain local intellectual activity has persisted there. We wish to locate this, and to afford it an outlet in literary expression.
>
> Exactly what that local temperament and artistic aptitude are, *Ulad* wants to discuss. *Ulad* would also influence them,

direct and inform them. And as the Theatre is the most essential of all art activities, and the surest test of a people's emotional and intellectual vitality, *Ulad* starts out as the organ of the Theatre, the Ulster Literary Theatre, but proposes to be as irrelevant to that movement and its topics as is deemed necessary. We intend to strike our keynote through the Theatre where our own plays will be produced, and to let that discover our pathway for us and voice those aims and hopes and hatreds and loves best expressed that way.

We recognise at the outset that our art of the drama will be different from that other Irish drama which speaks from the stage of the Irish National Theatre in Dublin, where two men, W. B. Yeats and Douglas Hyde, have set a model in Anglo-Irish and Gaelic plays with a success that is surprising and exhilarating. Dreamer, mystic, symbolist, Gaelic poet and propagandist have all spoken on the Dublin stage, and a fairly defined local school has been inaugurated. We in Belfast and Ulster also wish to set up a school; but there will be a difference.

At present we can only say that our talent is more satiric than poetic. That will probably remain the broad difference between the Ulster and the Leinster schools. But when our genius arrives, as he must sooner or later, there is no accounting for what extraordinary tendency he may display. Our business is, however, to plod along gathering matter for his use, practising methods, perfecting technique and training actors.

We hope to publish a short play with each number. These plays will all be by Ulster writers. A page or more will be devoted to Gaelic, and the rest of the magazine to essays, short poems, and illustrations ... we do not aim at being sixpence-worth; we aim at being priceless, for honesty and good purpose are priceless. If we do not attain to all this, we shall at least attain to something unique in Ulster, smacking of the soil, the winds on the uplands, the north coast, the sun and the rain, and the long winter evenings.

Ulad will be non-sectarian and non-political; each article will be signed by the writer as an expression of his own views; other views may be put forward in another number. In any case, our pages will be kept free from the party-cries of mob and clique and market-place. Our contributors are mostly young men, of all sects and all grades of political opinion. The journal will be run on broad propagandist lines. Propagandism on broad lines, we think, is desirable at this juncture. There is a strong undercurrent of culture in the North, and this we will endeavour to tap, and, if possible, turn into native channels. If we succeed in accomplishing this much, if we awaken the people to sympathy and life, surely our existence will be justified.[6]

Reynold's editorial, while guarded in tone and imprecise in expression, hints at a certain Ulster self-sufficiency. A short allegorical lyric 'Ulad', by Bulmer Hobson, that follows immediately, sees the mission of an awakened North symbolised in the wind that stirs and revives South, East and West. The first verse runs:

In the north is the strength of the wind, of the whirlwind;
In the south there are murmuring waters;
The east has a *caoine* for its song;
In the west is strengthless love.

Under the pen-name of William Donn, Reynolds contributed an article in which he viewed with foreboding the material from which the Theatre would have to shape its actors:

In order to understand our difficulty it is necessary to remember that we live in Belfast, that we are Presbyterian, or that we are Catholic or Episcopal with a hard layer of Presbyterian crudeness and repression upon top of that: and crudeness and repression are not good for the stuff out of which actors are to be made. Where every natural impulse has been dried up at its inception, all gaiety eyed with suspicion, all goodwill withdrawn lest it commit one to a little generous feeling, and all forms and ceremonies deemed unprofitable and vain, how can the necessary forgetfulness and self-abandonment exist that mimicry and pantomime demand? ... we owe certain mental, if not temperamental characteristics to the Scot ... and I should not here insist on his separateness but for psychological purposes, and to account for our comparative inability to play in drama ... in Dublin they have not this temperamental difficulty to contend against, and their results in a short time have been proportionately satisfactory.[7]

But in the beginning Dublin had much less confidence than the Belfast group in the abilities of the native actor. The Irish Literary Theatre's early productions of *The Heather Field*, *The Countess Cathleen* and *Maeve* were cast largely from English professionals recruited by George Moore. The Dublin critics agreed that English actors in Irish parts was incongruous. 'What is the use' cried Frank Fay 'of using the title "Irish" Literary Theatre if we have to get English actors because we are too lazy to train Irish ones?'[8] Apart from the flying visit of Quin and Digges in 1902, the Ulster Theatre from the beginning peopled its stage with its own members.

A mere twenty years before Reynolds voiced his fears, a great figure in the American theatre, John McCullough, died in Philadelphia. He had arrived in the United States a penniless youth from Dunboe in County Londonderry. In McCullough's genealogy may be found Cochranes, Wrays and McBlanes, all names to be read in the Kirk Sessions of Ulster. But hindsight, looking back over the last seventy years or so, informs us that, in the art of 'mimicry and pantomime', to be a Presbyterian is not a crippling disability. A closer look and we observe that it is not in our players but in our playwrights that the ability to express passion and love has burned low in the cool North.

The editorial in the first *Ulad* drew a protest in the second issue from a contributor, 'Connla', a pen-name said to be that of James Connolly. If this identification is correct the Irish labour leader must have submitted this article and one that appeared in the first *Ulad* from the United States where he lived from 1903 until 1910. Anyway, 'Connla's' rejoinder 'Festina Lente!' appeared in the Feil Brighde number of February 1905. What he had to say is important in that it reminds us again that this Theatre had been hafted and honed by Hobson, Purcell and their companions above all as a weapon of propaganda for a united Ireland.

'Connla' sees a danger in the suggestion that the U.L.T. should set up a 'school' in Belfast, such as Dublin has, but with a difference.

> Ulster has not yet sufficiently assimilated the rudiments of *national* culture on which she must base the development of her best *provincial* characteristics. If we accept the broad fact that Ireland, of which Ulster is a part, is a *nation*, we must recognise that provincial differences will be quantitative rather than qualitative ... the provincial self-consciousness which would arbitrarily define a 'school' while the elements of a possible 'school' are still in a state of flux, is less a matter for encouragement than deprecation, and to proclaim that attitude aloud to the four winds of Eire is scarcely becoming our modesty.

The Editor is also mistaken in asserting satire to be the predominant quality in the Northern group. In 'Connla's' opinion ...

> we can scarce claim satire, or the need of satire, an unique

possession. Dramatic satire demands a plasticity of temperament and a subtlety of word and wit, with which we do not find our average Ulsterman ordinarily gifted. I am not speaking of our dramatists, but of those whose lives afford the dramatic material. To mould their plays from their experience as typified in the Ulster Irishman is indeed a worthy aim; better defined as an attempt to realise Ulster to the rest of Ireland than to set up a new 'school' of dramatic art. It is a fallacious and fictitious originality which aims at being different from everything else extant. Let us labour patiently at our own material. If the product is really good . . . our identity and our differences will be simultaneously manifest.

'Connla' is knocking over an aunt sally of his own making. At the same time he gives Reynolds an opportunity to restate, after two years of existence, the objectives of the Ulster Theatre. In his second editorial he states:

We have not striven to erect a barrier between Ulster and the rest of Ireland; but we aim at building a citadel in Ulster for Irish thought and art achievements such as exists in Dublin. If the result is provincial rather than national it will not be our fault, but due to local influences over which we have no control. That the work in Ulster will for some time be of a critical and destructive nature, as well as constructive and creative, no one who knows the conditions will deny. Here our satire will come in. We have not attempted to define a school. To say that our talent in drama will be more satiric than otherwise is not defining a school, but merely stating what may be, and indeed is, a ruling characteristic. No, we shall have our own way, though the differences will always be within the generous circle of one nationality, just as local idiom may be, or the different character of the country and the coast, north, south, east or west, may be, and still be Ireland.[9]

W. B. Reynolds could speak with confidence. On 8 December 1904 the Ulster Literary Theatre had offered to the public its first two productions, written, acted, staged and produced by its members.

2

The Ulster Literary Theatre

(ii) PLAYS AND PLAYERS

'While Mr Purcell, in *The Reformers*, busies himself with modern Ireland, Mr Bulmer Hobson, in *Brian of Banba*, takes his subject from Ireland of the heroic age.' It was, no doubt, with a sense of achievement that these young men and women of the U.L.T. offered, in the first season under their new title, two plays which fulfilled the objectives of the Theatre; Purcell's comedy in which he exercised the desired 'satiric talent' and Hobson's poetic play on a Hero-King of an older Ireland. (This may have been fortuitous, for while Purcell's play was written for the U.L.T., Hobson's *Brian of Banba* had been published in *The United Irishman* in 1902. But Hobson was a founder of the Ulster Theatre, had expressed an opinion that they should write their own plays, and could well have written *Brian* in anticipation of the Theatre coming into being.)

Those early brief plays are not now available. Almost the only information we have of them is in the criticism of the productions by J. W. Good in *Ulad* of February 1905. Of *The Reformers*, a satire on municipal jobbery, Good comments that if Purcell's . . .

comedy sometimes becomes farce, his satire never degenerates into vulgar abuse. He handles his batch of rogues tenderly, as if he loved them; and his quiet and smiling irony is infinitely more effective than the loud-mouthed denunciations of the popular rhetorician ... Mr Purcell has given us a comedy remarkable not only for its own merits, but for the impetus it will lend to the movement for the formation of a new school of literary drama in Ulster.[1]

Bulmer Hobson, Good feels, had set himself the more difficult task. There was the inevitable comparison with the plays of Yeats ...

and there are few living poets who can bear the comparison unscathed. If in *Brian of Banba* the words do not 'sing and shine' as in *The King's Threshold*, if Mr Hobson's figures have not the austere simplicity and magic appeal of Mr Yeats' creations, yet he has drawn his inspiration from the same wells, and there is in his work something at once elemental and significant, 'beauty touched with strangeness'.

Altogether, this brief season in the Ulster Minor Hall was much more successful than the company's earlier ventures. The bill was played for two nights and attracted enough public support to justify a further run in the following week. For these performances music lent its aid to the other arts of the stage; an arrangement by Carl Hardebeck of the folk-tune 'The Lark in the Clear Air' was played as an intermission piece. As for the acting, J. W. Good felt that if it had not yet 'the spontaneity or the ripeness' of the Dublin theatre, yet

the performances ... proved once and for all that there is no real ground for the fears expressed by William Donn that the Ulster temperament would prove an insuperable bar to success on the stage. The ease and dignity with which the players performed their parts came as a pleasant surprise, and showed that in addition to the enthusiasm and good-will which one knew they would bring to the task, there was an unexpected reserve of dramatic power.[2]

Commenting on the performances of one or two actors, Good remarks that the names of the actors do not appear on the programme. According to Whitford Kane 'the company agreed at the outset that everything should be subordinated to the Theatre and that none of their names should appear on the programme'.[3] This practice was continued until 1908, when, on the company's first appearance at the old Theatre Royal, Belfast, the management insisted on the cast being shown.

One part of the Theatre's work Good could praise unreservedly—the staging and dressing of the production.

Even Mr Yeats who in this respect will not tolerate anything that falls far short of perfection, would, I think, have been pleased with Mr Jack Morrow's dressing and Mr Fred Morrow's staging of the piece. He would have admired their resolute preference for convention in place of a sham naturalism, the severe simplicity of the costumes and the skill with which they composed their colour scheme. *Brian of Banba* . . . was a poetic play staged as one had dreamt that poetic plays should be staged. The death bed of the King, with the flickering lights, the bowed heads of the wailing women, and the vague figures looming up against the dull-coloured draperies of the background, had in it the spirit of tragedy, and touched one as with a new revelation.[4]

Active in Belfast at the same time was a drama group run by the members of the School of Art Sketching Club and their friends. Among their theatrical offerings were Scribe's *The Ladies' Battle*, H. T. Craven's *Meg's Diversion*, and the 'famous comedies', *The Benicia Boy* and *Home*. There is no evidence that they were particularly interested in the Irish theatre. But, on the closing of the old Art School in 1904, the group joined forces with Purcell, Hobson, Campbell and Reynolds, bringing into the Ulster Literary Theatre men and women who were greatly to enrichen its fortunes and future. Among them were those fine actors, W. R. Gordon and James Hodgen, John McBurney 'who,' as Forrest Reid recalled, 'with Parkhill (Lewis Purcell), Reynolds and Good, by his personal influence did perhaps more for the cause of art in Belfast than anybody else,'[5] and Harry C. Morrow (Gerald MacNamara). MacNamara has recorded that:

> These men and women (they were all out of their teens) joined the Ulster Literary Theatre *en masse* and proved a great asset. There were no authors among them, but they had played before large audiences and always had a good Press. Being occupied in artistic professions outside acting, they were capable of painting scenery, making props, drawing posters, designing costumes and other things which were helpful in the Theatre.[6]

If the Abbey Theatre had its Fay brothers the Ulster company had its Morrows. All the Theatre's activities without exception were affected by their energy and genius. Jack, Edwin and Fred acted or staged or produced, Norman, another artist member of the family, contributed three interesting drawings of members of the company to the first number of *Ulad*. Harry, under the pen-name of Gerald MacNamara, was one of the two outstanding playwrights of the U.L.T. No account of the Theatre can ignore the work of Fred Morrow who was its producer for thirty years. In a B.B.C. radio feature on the Ulster Literary Theatre,[6] broadcast some years ago, former members of the company recorded their recollections of Fred's methods. His son, George Morrow, commented on the seeming casualness of his approach: 'He apparently didn't work from any plan, any preconceived idea. He seemed to carry everything in his head and yet from one rehearsal to the other he could . . . remember sufficiently to keep an actor in the proper position, in the right intonation and so on.' Kitty Murphy, a well-known actress with the company thought that Fred Morrow was 'A unique producer. He would appear not to be interested at all, then he would suddenly have a flash of inspiration and would really bring something quite different out of the play.' But Jack Gavin, who appeared in many of the Theatre's productions, recalled that Fred did a lot of home-work before rehearsals: 'When we were doing a new play he used to bring down a miniature theatre with all the characters in it, all in their proper perspectives and all in their proper places.'

The Theatre was faithfully served by people whose names rarely appeared on the playbills. Simon O'Leary, a Belfast business man, worked enthusiastically behind scenes, some-times as prompter, sometimes in the box office. J. Field Magee was for years secretary, later stage manager. Padraig Gregory, although he was to win recognition in later years as a poet, never wrote for the Theatre, but served it as treasurer. Years later Dr Gregory remembered how he was brought into contact with the company:

> I was introduced to the Ulster Theatre because Purcell and I both served our apprenticeship in the same architect's office. He collared me into the movement by way of making me a ticket-collector or programme-seller, or whatever you like. He brought me round to the places where these plays were being produced, put me at the door, and told me to collect all the money that I could.

It was about this time, early in the history of the Theatre,

that Rutherford Mayne was introduced to its work, again by
the indefatigable Purcell.

One night in digs Purcell suddenly appeared and induced me
to buy tickets to go and see the society that he was interested
in. They were performing, so far as my recollection goes,
A.E.'s *Deirdre* and Yeats' *Cathleen Ni Houlihan*, and I
distinctly remember Padraig Gregory sitting like Peter at the
receipt of custom when we went in.

There was a sparse audience. But I was very interested by
Deirdre, more than by *Cathleen*, because I had been a great
admirer of what you might call rhetorical stuff such as actors
love. I'm afraid I didn't quite catch what Yeats was at
because the audience seemed to take it as a sort of rather
funny peasant play. The beauty of the words was all lost
because the acting was so bad, to tell you the honest truth.
But I was struck by *Deirdre* and particularly by two actors
in it, John and Joseph Campbell. They had magnificent
voices, and they filled my idea of how a man should speak
verse.[7]

But it is from Forrest Reid, in many ways an onlooker, that
we gain our most intimate glimpse into the workings of the
U.L.T., early in 1905, as they prepare for their second season
of productions, Purcell's *The Enthusiast* and *The Little
Cowherd of Slaigne* by Joseph Campbell. As we know, it was
through W. B. Reynolds that Reid made acquaintance with
the U.L.T. Reynolds, says Reid, 'saw with the eye of faith' and
on the strength of the first two or three productions was
already discussing architectural plans for a threatre and schemes
for a building fund. Forrest Reid writes:

It was to no such Temple of the Muses, however, that he
took me on this damp dark night of January or February,
1905, but to a house in May Street, and there, in a brightly-
lit and extremely chilly back room upstairs, I watched a

rehearsal of *The Enthusiast*. Fred Morrow was stage managing; and W. R. Gordon was there, and Bulmer Hobson, and John Campbell, the black-and-white artist, who played the part of Sam McKinstry, and Jack Morrow, whose acting as James McKinstry, the enthusiast, was to my mind (still filled with the so much more glowing enthusiasm of Reynolds) the one weak spot in the piece . . . Rutherford Mayne, who had the part of Rab, the servant man, was not present, but Good came in later, and John McBurney, who with Parkhill (Purcell), Reynolds and Good, by his personal influence did perhaps more for the cause of art in Belfast than anybody else. Of the acting, I remember principally Gordon's very fine interpretation of William John McKinstry, the old farmer; but the whole thing was a revelation to me, it was so fresh, natural, and new, and I felt that Reynolds, after all, had not exaggerated its importance. I still believe *The Enthusiast* to be a genuine work of art—slight, imperfect, but vital.[8]

Purcell's *The Enthusiast*, and Joseph Campbell's *The Little Cowherd of Slaigne*, were produced in the Clarence Place Hall on 4–6 May 1905. Once again a play drawn from Irish mythology shared the bill with a 'realistic' play; a phenomenon as evident then in Dublin as in Belfast. Reading now the story of how those plays were written this recurring pattern seems to have been fortuitous rather than the deliberate policy of either of the Theatres. It was suggested that Campbell, like Hobson in the previous season, had written his play in imitation of Yeats. But, remembering the idealogical origins of the Ulster Theatre, it is as reasonable to think that the Ulster writers, living in a community indifferent or openly hostile to their aspirations, strove to recall the heroic Gaelic past, even if Campbell never fully cleared the lesser faery world of malign leprechaun and changeling.

But the Ulster Literary Theatre was not to belong to the poets. Joseph Campbell was vitally interested in poetry as an oral art; he was, by all accounts, an actor of fine voice and presence. Today his considerable reputation rests on his poetry, not on his playwriting. *The Little Cowherd* was published in the first number of *Ulad* and *The Enthusiast* in Number Three, the Beltain issue of May 1905. In the fourth, and what was to be the final issue of the journal, the Lughnasa number of September 1905, there appeared a review of the plays, with three illustrations by Norman Morrow of characters from *The Enthusiast*. The criticism was written by Joseph Power (Seosamh de Paor) and he deals briefly if kindly with Campbell's play:

> That Seosamh Mac Cathmhaoil can produce good work is indisputable; that he has not done so in this little picture of ancient Ireland is equally so . . . the dialogue is, for the most part, too ornate, with here and there sentences of extreme colloquialism. The long and the short of it is that Seosamh Mac Cathmhaoil has not yet found himself, and he never will attain to the knowledge whilst he sails such shadowy waters.

The critic of the *Irish News* also noted this incongruity in Campbell's dramatic dialogue. On the audience's part 'there was a slight tendency to regard Ferghal, the dog boy, as a sort of comic relief, a tendency accentuated by the colloquialism of some of his lines.' The *Northern Whig* critic paying a tribute to Campbell 'as a writer of graceful and original verse' felt that the tragedy of Fionnghuala, the King's daughter, lured to her death by the wiles of the magical and malevolent Cowherd 'stirs us too much as a picture or a narrative, and not with the living and passionate gesture of life.' All three critics spoke

enthusiastically of the acting of the women in Campbell's play
and of Fred Morrow's staging and sets.

In the *Northern Whig* report there is an assessment of the
U.L.T.'s work, valuable because it is one of the few contemporary comments outside the pages of *Ulad*:

> Even those who do not agree with the tendencies of the
> Theatre must admit that it stands for an ideal and it is all too
> seldom that one finds an ideal governing an amateur
> dramatic performance. For the most part amateurs are
> content to be sedulous mimics of professional performers
> without any attempt to capture the illusion of life or stir the
> spectator by the display of beautiful and expressive emotions
> ... but the Ulster Literary Theatre does pursue a deliberate
> and remote ideal that in itself serves to lift them out of the
> ruck of ordinary companies and ensures that they must be
> judged by a higher and more severe standard.[9]

The aims of the U.L.T. had never at any time been other
than idealistic. Now, with the production of Purcell's play,
they ensured that they would, in future, be judged by other
standards as a *theatre*. The Enthusiast of the play is James
McKinstry, home on holidays on his father's farm in County
Antrim. His mind is 'full of a great work.' He is filled with
enthusiasm for the revolutionary idea of co-operative farming
and tries to communicate it to the family—his father, his Aunt
Marget, his brother Sam, and Rab, the labouring man.
'Suppose', he begins, 'suppose now a dozen farmers agreed to
combine their farms and work them on a large scale, as they do,
for instance, in America. You would find that it could be made
to pay with one-half the sum of the work that is expended on
the separate dozen farms. Do you follow me?'

FATHER: Weel—I don't know—just at the minute. I wud

3

need to think it ower a bit. I'm—I'm no sure about it, Jamie.

RAB: (*reading the local paper, laughs aloud. Sam turns and asks him what it is about*)

JAMES: But I'm sure about it, father. I intend to call a meeting of the countryside and lay the scheme before them.

FATHER: A meetin'?

SAM: In the Orange Hall?

JAMES: No, no. It can't be in the Orange Hall . . . you see, it wouldn't do to have it there. We want *everybody* into this. Neither Home Ruler nor Catholics would come to it. I'll hold it in the big meadow.

SAM: Home Rulers in it?

AUNT: (*throwing down* The Christian Herald) An' Catholics? Lord 'a mercy!

FATHER: Jamie, lad, I doubt—doubt—

AUNT: A meeting o' Home Rulers in *our* meadow. Lord 'a mercy.

JAMES: (*exasperated*) Oh, how long is this damnable division of the people to last? This miserable suspicion!

RAB: (*reaching over* The Budget *to Sam*) It's dam' good this week. There's three murders in it. I'll hae to go an' cut them turmits.

(*Rab goes out. Sam buries himself in* The Budget. *Aunt Marget is reading* The Christian Herald. *Father dozes*)

JAMES: But I will carry it through. I will bring all creeds and classes together on a common platform and allow them to learn by practical experience that—

(he stops, seeing that no one is listening. Sam, reading, chuckles to himself. Father snores)

JAMES: I am alone in this.

And the curtain descends on the first act. The meeting is convened in McKinstry's big meadow. James addresses his neighbours 'for near han' an hour.' Rab is unable to give Aunt Marget a fuller report, for, as he admits, 'I wuz cracking the whole time to a wheen o' girls.' 'Irishmen', writes A. E. Malone, 'are too much in earnest to laugh merely for the sake of laughing, always they are trying either to improve the community of which they are a part, or they are trying to wound their neighbours by laughing at them.'[10]

Purcell, the satirist, satisfies his anger and laughter on James McKinstry's audience. In a brief but vivid second scene he drags into the daylight their arrogance, ignorance and obscurantism. Hughey Gibb takes the Enthusiast's place on the platform and asks: 'If they were going to bring in a' sorts o' machinery for to do the work, what wuz going to become o' the poor labourers?' A reasonable enough query, but old Andy Moore is more to the taste of one section of the meeting when he declares: 'they were going till upset the Crown and Constitution. An' at the wind-up he axed Jamie if he cud gie Scripture for it, an' Jamie as much as said he cudn't. Then somebody shouted "Socialism," and Ned Graham—he wuz drunk—he shouted it wuz a Fenian thing, and he kept shoutin' that the whole time.'

The meeting breaks up in confusion and violence, or, as Rab has it: 'Oh, it wuz a grand meeting. I never seen a better fight'. And Aunt Marget knows where to lay the blame: 'What else cud ye expect but a fight, bringin' Home Rulers and Catholics, and Dippers, and tramps, an' a' the riff-raff o' the country into the same field. It's flyin' in the face o' Providence![11]

James, safely back in the house, reflects on the debacle and
decides that 'I might carry it out yet—in spite of everything.'
Then he hears the cheers of the mob and the mutter of the
drums. He sinks back, defeated, and the drums are answered by
Rab's loutish laughter from the next room.

It is probable that Purcell was influenced in his choice of
theme by Sir Horace Plunkett's co-operative farming movement, The Irish Agricultural Organisation, founded in 1901.
Commenting on a revival of the play on 19 May 1909, the
Northern Whig thought the comedy was 'doubly appropriate
now that the co-operative idea is being carried over the
province like a fiery cross . . . Sir Horace Plunkett might do
worse than subsidise the Literary Theatre to produce it in
districts which up to the present have remained deaf to his
gospel.'

The deafness of the Enthusiast's neighbours and his defeat
moved Padraic Colum, on seeing the play performed by the
London branch of the Dungannon Club, to describe it as 'an
immoral play' because it 'showed no door of hope opening to
the idealist and his dreams.'[12] But if Purcell found more
dramatic potential in the politics than the economics of his
story, to Ulster theatregoers *The Enthusiast* was significant
because for the first time the contemporary Ulster countryman
strode the stage. In the summer of 1905 the U.L.T. took *The
Enthusiast* and *Brian of Banba* to a Feis at Toome Bridge, in
County Antrim. Cathal O'Shannon, the writer and journalist,
was in the audience. Years later he recalled what a revelation
that visit of the U.L.T. was to an impressionable schoolboy:

The only plays that I had ever seen at that age, and in a
country town, Draperstown in County Derry, were by
local amateurs. They generally played Boucicault—plays
like the *The Shaughran*, or an occasional English farce like

Box and Cox. But when I saw this performance in Toome Bridge, even though I was only a youngster of thirteen years of age, I was very much impressed. I was interested enough in *Brian of Banba*, because I knew the story . . . but what really did impress me was *The Enthusiast*, because for the first time I saw the kind of people that I knew and lived among in Co. Antrim and Co. Derry were there alive and talking as they talked at home.[13]

In his article in the *Times*, Forrest Reid said of Purcell's play that it was 'in one way perhaps more vital than anything the Ulster Theatre has produced since, for we must remember that from it sprang the more significant of the only two forms of drama it has yet mastered, folk-comedy and fantastic farce'.

For these productions Reid's friend, W. B. Reynolds, with Carl Hardebeck, offered the audience 'a pleasing innovation, an excellent string band, which beguiled the intervals of waiting,' a fact worth mentioning if only to record that one of the artistes was Cahal O'Byrne, a man held in affection by Belfast citizens of a past generation.

Much of the enduring worth of *The Enthusiast* lies in its use of country idiom. In his review in *Ulad*, Joseph Power offers the surprising information that 'since I first read Mr Purcell's play, the author has rewritten it in dialect,' and continues: 'he has caught the idiom more cleverly than any previous writer.' But Purcell, having mastered this racy dialogue language, turned for his next play, *The Pagan*, to sixth-century Ireland. Ernest A. Boyd describes it as 'an amusing comedy . . . where the humorous aspect of the struggle between Paganism and Christianity finds expression in the Pagan choice of a young Christian girl wooed by many suitors. It is the only play which attempts to visualise in comedic form the competition of two opposite moral tendencies in ancient Ireland.'[14] On the evidence of Purcell's earlier plays, an interpretation equally plausible is that *The Pagan*, a satire rather than a tale of heroes, deals with problems nearer in time; the 'mixed marriage' and the collision between parsimonious puritanism and 'the sweet wild times' that the Ulsterman, with a vague unease, feels must have existed sometime, somewhere.

It was left to a young actor, Rutherford Mayne, who had won plaudits as Rab in Purcell's earlier play, to bring back the countryman to the Theatre's stage. With *The Pagan*, Mayne's *Turn of the Road* was produced early in December 1906 in the Hall of Queen's College, Belfast, under the auspices of the Literary and Scientific Society. A few days later (17–19 Dec.), the same bill was presented at the Ulster Minor Hall. In the following Spring, 30 March 1907, the U.L.T. took the two plays to Dublin, the first of many visits to the Abbey Theatre. Joseph Holloway's entry on that occasion reads: 'I have not enjoyed myself so much at a theatre for a very long time as at the Abbey tonight in witnessing the first performance in Dublin of the Ulster Literary Theatre. What struck me most was the fine physique of the players when compared with all in the N.T.S. The lovers and heroic characters were fine fellows to look upon and not like puppets of a pigmy race. What the company lacks is finish; the players have talent and plenty to spare.'[15] The Dublin productions, attended by W. B. Yeats, Lady Gregory and Douglas Hyde, were successful and within the year *The Pagan* and *The Turn of the Road* had appeared under the imprint of Maunsel and Company of Dublin. These were the first U.L.T. plays to be published.

In *The Turn of the Road*, a play in two scenes and an epilogue, Rutherford Mayne is generally held to be depicting the conflict between the artist and a puritanical community. The central character is Robbie John Granahan, a young violinist of talent.

His family regard his preoccupation with music as unworthy of a man, a folly in a farmer. The play is set 'in a farm kitchen of the present day'. To call this Granahan household with its loveless, mean-spirited inhabitants 'puritanical' seems a sad misuse of the word. Discussing the play some years ago, the author said to me: 'I don't think I saw *The Turn of the Road* as an assault against puritanism, for which, no doubt, something good might be said, but against a pervasive evil in Ireland, philistinism, for which nothing good whatsoever can be said.'

But the play, powerful and appealing for all its faults, is not peopled solely by ingrates. There is Robbie John's sweetheart, Jane Graeme, who, unlike the girl in Purcell's *The Enthusiast*, encourages her lover in his quest. 'Take that fiddle,' she says 'and do what your heart tells you to ... God made you a musician and not a farmer.' There is the tramp with his Cremona who stepped down long ago from the rostrum of the 'Blue Bohemian Wind and String Band,' and is driven away now from the Granahan hearth. And when Robbie John is in turn cast out into the storm and darkness there is the Grandfather who turns to castigate the father:

GRANDFATHER: Ye thought he was wasting time and money. D'ye think there's nothing in this life beyond making money above the rent? I tell you it's not the money alone that makes life worth living. It's the wee things ye think nothing of, but that makes your home a joy to come back till, after a hard day's work ... And you've sent out into the could and wet the one that was making your home something more than the common. D'ye think them proud city folk will listen to his poor ould ballads with the heart of the boy singing through them ... it's only us, I say, could listen him in the right way. And ye knowed, right well ye knowed, that every

string of his fiddle was keyed to the crying of your own
heart.

WILLIAM JOHN: (*half sobbing*) There, there, God forgive me
. . . I did na know. Maybe if I say a word or two—Oh, God
forgive us this night our angry words, and have mercy on
my wayward son, O Lord, and keep him safe from harm,
and deliver him not unto the adversary.

GRANDFATHER: Amen. Aye. Aye. Ye done well, Let not
the sun go down upon your wrath.

WILLIAM JOHN: (*going to door*) It's a coorse night. I'll leave
the door on the hesp. (*he unbolts the door*)[16]

(CURTAIN)

The door of the U.L.T. was, from now on, most certainly
left on the latch and one of the first to enquire what lay within
was the distinguished Irish actor, Whitford Kane. Kane's
memoirs, *Are We All Met?*, in which he recounts his distinguished professional theatrical career in Ireland, England and the
United States appeared in 1931. How, shortly after the production of *The Turn of the Road*, he 'came under the spell of the
Ulster Theatre' he narrates as follows:

Up to this time my entire theatrical experience had been in
English playhouses and I knew hardly anything about the
Abbey and the Ulster Theatres. This may seem strange, but
things Irish were not very popular in a northern town like
Belfast, which had always looked towards England for all
things cultural . . . However, an Ulsterman can never quite
escape his national birthright and so before very long I had
to face the issue.

It is to my affiliation with the Ulster Literary Theatre and
to Rutherford Mayne in particular that I am indebted for
finding myself. One evening during one of my summer

vacations he took me to see his first play, *The Turn of the Road*, which was being acted in the Ulster Hall, Belfast. This performance must have struck some national chord in me for I went again the next night; after that I was asked to join a gathering at the Arts Club. There I heard for the first time some of the beautiful folksongs and poems of my own country, and, as I listened to them, I realised how Irish I really was and also how intensely Irish Ulster was in spite of its many peculiar distinctions.[17]

Rutherford Mayne gained some professional experience touring with Kane and the Mollison Company in 1908. Kane recalls that 'Mayne, did not, however, stick to acting but returned to Ireland to his Government post.'

The Turn of the Road had been dedicated to Lewis Purcell. In 1907, Purcell with Gerald Macnamara (Harry C. Morrow) produced a fantastic burlesque, *Suzanne and the Sovereigns*, that was to carry the name of the Theatre far beyond Belfast. The play began as a Christmas burlesque staged some years earlier at the Morrow home in North Queen Street, Belfast. The Morrow family, as H. L. Morrow recalls 'had the extraordinary advantage of having large business premises (in Clifton Street) where they had showrooms on various levels, and the result is that the whole business premises was turned into a theatre at Christmas holidays.' A note in the U.L.T. Scrapbook, quoted by Dr McHenry, states that:

A play called *Suzanne* was written in 1900 by George Morrow, Norman Morrow and Harry C. Morrow and produced before a small private audience . . . taking part, John Campbell, John McBurney, W. R. Gordon, Sam Miller, George, Edwin, Fred, Jack, Norman and Harry C. Morrow. In the summer of 1907, David Parkhill (Lewis Purcell) and Harry C. Morrow (Gerald Macnamara) wrote a play . . .

based on *Suzanne*, but entirely rewritten. Morrow wrote 1st and 2nd acts and one scene of 3rd act. David Parkhill wrote the remainder and he, (D.P.), produced it in the Exhibition Hall, 1907.[18]

The Sovereigns of *Suzanne* are King William and King James. As Rutherford Mayne wrote:

Morrow had the audacity to make one of the principal characters of the play no less a personage than King William the Third of 'glorious, pious and immortal memory.' The part was taken by Norman, whose appearance on the stage was an almost exact reproduction in features and attire of the conventional portrait . . . on hundreds of Orange banners. The reason for William's advent in Ulster was given as due to the impassioned appeal of a deputation from Sandy Row to save the daughter of their local Grand Master from the unwelcome attentions of King James. Fortunately, what might have been the cause of a first-class riot was turned by irresistible wit and humour into an uproarious success.

Three years later, following a production of *Suzanne and the Sovereigns* at the Grand Opera House, Belfast, the critic of the *Ulster Guardian* (26 November 1910) was still amazed not to 'learn from some frightened official that the theatre was besieged.' The only protest seems to have been occasioned by the programmes sold at the January 1909 production. These were printed as broadsheets with a drawing by John Campbell of King William astride a rocking horse. For subsequent productions a drawing of martial trophies was substituted. The ballad that follows does not identify the actors but supplies brief character sketches of the dramatis personae:

> William Three, a hero-king
> Brave and kind and good look-ing.
> James the Second. For him see

Note above on William Three.
Sweet Suzanne. A maiden fair—
Pearly teeth and golden hair.
Lundy, traitor, villain, spy,
Bold and bad and very sly.
Wilhelm Jan Van Tootil, Great
Banner painter to the State.
First is, Francey J. McCann
Second, William Kernahan
Third, Sir Joseph Prendergast;
Deputation from Belfast.[19]

Then follow descriptions of Admiral Genkle, the Duke of
Schomberg, Lord Tyrconnel and Colonel Kelly of the Jacobite
army, concluding with:

Soldiers, sailors—nicely dressed;
Citizens and all the rest.

Anticipating criticism of this remarkable confrontation on
the grounds of improbability, the authors state on the broad-
sheet that:

members of the audience who may be inclined to dismiss
certain scenes and incidents as resting on no basis of historical fact are requested to suspend judgment until, in
addition to the works of popular authors like Macauley,
Lecky, Froude and Leland, they have carefully studied and
collated the undermentioned authorities:—

Among the long list of publications that the playgoer is
urged to consult are: *Journal of the House of Commons of
Ireland,* 1613–1800 (19 vols. folio), Cane's *History of William-
ite and Jacobite Wars in Ireland, Collectanea de rebus Hibernias,*
Howell's *State Trials* (15 vols.), Zeuss' *Grammatica Celtica,
Irish Auxiliary of the London Society for Promoting Christianity
among the Jews—Third Annual Report* (Dublin, 1821).

Suzanne and the Sovereigns opened in the Exhibition Hall on the last week of December 1907. On the first night the improvised stage was set up about the centre of the hall. But news of this delirious version of the Orange and Green feud got abroad. By New Year's Eve, the end of the run, the stage was against the far wall and the house was packed with an enthusiastic audience. The U.L.T. had had its first popular success.

For the revival of the play at the Exhibition Hall in January 1909 Macnamara rewrote and reshaped part of the script and new costumes were supplied by Whitford Kane. The incidental music for the production was composed by Carl Hardebeck, A. G. Potter and W. B. Reynolds. The opening music 'Overture 1690', is credited to Reynolds. Based on tunes such as 'The Boyne Water' and 'The Boys of Wexford', it seems to have been as witty and entertaining as the extravaganza.

The U.L.T. visited the Abbey Theatre again on 24–25 April 1908, taking with them two new plays, *The Leaders of the People* by Robert Harding and *The Drone* by Rutherford Mayne. In his *Times* article of 5 December 1922, Forrest Reid identified 'Robert Harding' as James Winder Good. Although it had a satisfactory Press, his 'electioneering play' does not seem to have been revived by the Theatre.

The players and their plays were received in Dublin with acclamation. The *Irish Times* critic wrote:

> Dublin must look to its laurels, for in art, as in everything else, when Ulster makes up its mind to try, the rest of Ireland is hard put to it to beat it . . . Both the plays and the acting are so remarkable that we may say without exaggeration that no more significant production has been seen in Dublin in our day. We seem to be on the verge of a revolution in dramatic art, and remarkably enough, it has been left to Ulster to lead the way.

In the opinion of the journal *Sinn Fein*, '*The Drone* is a master-piece of comedy of life and manners, the finest of its kind . . . that has ever yet been put on any Irish stage by Irish players.'[20]

W. B. Yeats did not see the U.L.T. on their second visit to Dublin but in November of that year he wrote:

> I remember vividly the performance of a year ago, the absence of the ordinary conventions, the novelty of move-ment and intonation . . . It was in their mechanism that their playwrights failed. It was in their delight in the details of life that they interested one. I hear, however, that their plays upon their last visit showed much more unity. In any case it is only a matter of time, where one finds so much sincere observation, for the rest to follow . . . the Ulster Players are the only dramatic society, apart from our own, which is doing serious artistic work.[21]

The Drone as originally produced at the Abbey was a play in two acts and this version was repeated by the U.L.T. at the Exhibition Hall, Belfast, 2–7 November 1908. This was a busy season for Rutherford Mayne. He had been on tour with the Mollison Company but found time to write a one-act tragedy, *The Troth*, and add a third act to *The Drone*. There is some doubt as to when the three-act version of *The Drone* was first produced. It seems likely that it was in the Belfast Opera House on 17–22 May 1909. Certainly it was in this form that the comedy achieved its astonishing popularity on the Irish stage. It has been said that Mayne reconstructed it to satisfy the need expressed years earlier in the third number of *Ulad* for a full-length play. But as he himself has explained it was drawn from the material of an earlier, unsuccessful play. He wrote a play, he recalled,

> a very long thing of about three acts, and the main character in it was an old harbour master who never did anything

right . . . ships went bumping into the wharf and all sorts of things of that description. And then I remember two old brothers, one kept a shop and he kept a brother, and the brother was what would be called a 'spoiled priest'. He had been at the Divinity Schools in Belfast and he never qualified; I suppose he could never get through the Hebrew. So it was these two old brothers and the harbour master. I threw aside the three-act play and the only remains of it would be *The Drone*.[22]

Doubtless the idiosyncrasies of all three originals can be traced in the comedy. No more than a brief summary is needed of the story of the two brothers of the play; John Murray, the hardworking County Down farmer and his 'lodger', Daniel the Drone, who, at the mention of hard work, retires to his den where he is believed to be inventing 'a new kind of fan-bellows' that will make everybody's fortune. The play has been published and republished.[23] In the length and breadth of Ireland there must be few dramatic societies which have not staged *The Drone*, and many times at that. It has passed into folklore. John McBride, the Ulster actor, recalls that when he first appeared in it he expressed an uneasiness about his lines to the producer, Fred Morrow. 'Don't worry', Morrow reassured him, 'if you need a prompt the audience will prompt you!'

Rutherford Mayne had toured a season with the William Mollison Company. Mollison now returned the compliment by bringing his company to Ireland. At the Theatre Royal, Belfast, on 11 November 1908 he presented Ian Maclaren's *The Bonnie Brier Bush* with Mayne's *The Troth* as a curtain-raiser. (This one-act play with Whitford Kane in the cast had been first produced by Mollison at the Crown Theatre, Peckham, London, in October 1908. It appeared in the U.L.T. repertory during the first season at the Grand Opera House, Belfast, beginning 17 May 1909.)

The Troth, the hurried and desperate pact between two rent-racked, starving cottiers, the Catholic Moore and the Protestant McKie, to assassinate their landlord, was a vastly different offering from the genial humour of *The Drone* or even *The Turn of the Road*. It would seem that the robust stomach of the Ulster playgoer of those days asked for sustenance other than the never-ending laugh. In this play, by revealing the essential unity of men under oppression regardless of religion, Mayne returned to the ideals that inspired the Theatre's founders. It was received almost everywhere with praise. '*The Troth* grips like great music', declared the *Belfast Telegraph*. 'It has the same innocent utterance. It will in a day or two receive adequate recognition from everyone; perhaps not for the right reasons in some cases, but in the majority for its sheer simple strength and beauty as tragic drama.' 'Mr Mayne's former experiments were in the vein of comedy', said the *Northern Whig*, 'but in *The Troth* he employs a tragic motive, handling it with power, directness, and refreshing realism. The characters owe nothing to tradition.' It was on this latter point that the play was faulted by 'M.O'D', the critic of the *Dublin Evening Mail*, who described it as 'Mid-Victorian Irish medodrama . . . deserving no place in the literature of Irish life.' The author's picture of ' "the distressful Irish peasant"—dating from the tradition we had hoped was finally exploded, of the Carleton-Lever school —is completely irrelevant to Irish life at present.' This drew a vigorous reply from Padraic Colum, who, courteously enlightening 'M.O'D.' on the difference in origin and stand-point of Carleton and Lever in Irish life, proceeds, 'I have often said that I regarded Rutherford Mayne as possessing the most dramatic instinct of any Irish dramatist . . . the Victorian era was Ireland's most tragic period. Then were those widespread evictions . . . Mr Rutherford Mayne has been fortunate in his period and his subject.'

* * *

With the burgeoning of Rutherford Mayne and Gerald Macnamara the U.L.T. entered a new phase. The theatre business in Belfast discovered that this amalgam of playwrights, actors, designers, producers and musicians was to be taken seriously. In 1909 when *Suzanne and the Sovereigns* was at the Exhibition Hall, Edward Terry was playing to very poor houses at the Opera House. The manager, investigating the reason for this lack of support for such a noted actor, discovered *Suzanne*. He promptly offered the U.L.T. a week's engagement at the Opera House, an association that was to last until 1934.

This widening of venue brought about a small but significant change in the Theatre's policy. According to Whitford Kane 'the company agreed at the outset that everything should be subordinated to the theatre and that none of their names should appear in the programme.' There was another reason for this anonymity, the attitude of certain sections of Belfast public opinion to 'playactors', for, as Kane reminds us, the members 'were men and women who followed their ordinary occupations during the day and devoted their leisure to the theatre.'[24] In the five years from 1904 to 1909 it is unlikely, of course, that the Press critics remained unaware of the identity of the actors. Yet, with one exception, they appear to have respected this rule of the Theatre. The exception, an interesting one, for it names some of the earliest players, appeared in *The Stage* for 15 December 1904. In a review of Hobson's *Brian of Banba* and Purcell's *Reformers*, we find the names of John P., Joseph and Josephine Campbell, Jack Morrow, W. R. Gordon, George

Merne, Sam Waddell and Bulmer Hobson himself.

But the management of the Grand Opera House could not accept nameless performers appearing before their patrons. The following is the programme presented by the U.L.T. at the Grand Opera House on 17 May 1909. Where possible I have appended the actor's real name; some I have failed to identify.

THE ENTHUSIAST—Lewis Purcell

William John McKinstry	J. M. Harding (James Hodgen)
James	Jackson Graham
Sam	Ross Canmer (John P. Campbell)
Aunt Marget	Miss Margaret O'Gorman (Bridie O'Farrell)
Minnie	Miss Maire Crothers
Rab	G. A. Charters

THE TROTH—Rutherford Mayne

Ebenezer McKie	Charles Kerr (later Charles K. Ayre)
Mrs McKie	Miss Seveen Canmer (Josephine Campbell)
Francis Moore	Ross Canmer
John Smith	Frank Dornan

THE TURN OF THE ROAD—Rutherford Mayne

William John Granahan .	Robert Gorman (W. R. Gordon)
Mrs Granahan	Miss Margaret O'Gorman
Samuel James	Rutherford Mayne
Robbie John	Ross Canmer
Ellen	Miss Maire Crothers

4

Thomas Granahan	. . . G. A. Charters
John Graeme	. . . . . . Gerald Macnamara
Jane.	. . . . Miss Seveen Canmer
Mr Taylor	. . . . . . John Field (J. F. Magee)
A tramp Fiddler	. . . . . James Dermody

For over thirty years almost every Ulster actor of note appeared at some time in the Theatre's productions. They included A. Gilmer, Sam Bulloch (the original Drone), R. H. Leighton, J. Storey, George Sayers, Fred Hughes, Edith Lilburn, Kitty Murphy, Walter Kennedy, Marion Crimmons, Rose McQuillan, Jean Woods and Jack Gavin. There are, no doubt, many other names that could be listed here. Some of them appear in later chapters of the history of Ulster drama. The actor, it has been said, is a sculptor who carves in snow and it is worthwhile, therefore, setting down the names of those men and women who interpreted so admirably the work of the playwrights. That this is so is evident from the reviews of cross-channel critics who saw the Theatre on tour and were not obliged to be generous in their comment. Francis Birrell was in a tiny minority when he wrote of the U.L.T.'s productions at the New Scala Theatre, London, that 'the Ulster Players are as provincial as their plays. Their chief accomplishment is the manipulation of a singularly barbarous dialect.'[25]

It was Whitford Kane who introduced the U.L.T. to English audiences. A staunch admirer of Rutherford Mayne as playwright and actor, Kane arranged a special matinee of *The Troth* at the Maiden Lane Theatre, London, in 1910. At Kane's invitation the production was attended by Barrie, Galsworthy, Granville-Barker and Pinero. Galsworthy had already heard of the Ulster playwright's work, probably through Kane, and in December of the preceding year had written to Mayne:

It has been a great pleasure to read your plays. I have sent *The Troth* on to Barrie. I hope it will be found possible to play it at the Duke of York's, though I fear there is rather a plethora of one act plays for the present opportunities of giving short plays.

With all good wishes. (Go on—you will do fine work),

I am,

Yours sincerely,

John Galsworthy.[26]

Whitford Kane was eager to take the U.L.T. on an English tour. In 1911 he arranged a short season at Kelly's Theatre, Liverpool. Then he discovered that not all the cast were free to travel. 'My actors were all employed', he writes, 'and my task was to pry them loose from their domestic moorings long enough to switch them over to Liverpool for a week and back. I interviewed the heads of concerns . . . and practically bribed them to let their employees enjoy a dramatic holiday.'[27] As Marion Crimmons recalled with characteristic humour, some of the moorings were closely domestic: 'I got on because I wasn't very religious, and it wasn't a sin to play on the stage. Whitford Kane had gone round until he was dog-tired, asking all the different mothers. "Oh, no, they wouldn't allow their girls to go to Liverpool, a place they didn't know!" '

However, Kane got a company together, 'The Ulster Players', and their bill which included *The Turn of the Road*, *The Drone*, *The Enthusiast* and *The Troth*, opened in Liverpool on the week of 8 May 1911, with a matinee in Manchester. Plays and players were well received. Speeches at curtain calls by both Rutherford Mayne and Whitford Kane were necessary every evening before the audiences were satisfied.

But, as Kane tells us in his autobiography:

Though most of the troupe were splendid in the peasant roles of the play, none of them had any sense of professional responsibility. It fell to me to see that no one strayed off for a walk just as the bus was ready to go into Liverpool, and again I had to be on the alert to see that no one escaped before we reached the theatre. I had a terrible time and felt like a hen with a flock of ducks.

Of the matinee at the Gaiety, Manchester, he adds, 'I would have tried more, but the strain of guiding my flock across provincial England was too much to permit of more than one attempt.'

Kane was determined, however, that London should see the Ulster Players in *The Drone* and he arranged matinees at the Royalty Theatre in February 1912. There the comedy was seen by William A. Brady, the American manager and partner of the Shuberts, who bought it for the United States. After trials at Washington and Baltimore, *The Drone* opened at Daly's Theatre, New York, on 30 December 1912, to play only two performances. Kane accuses Brady of 'Boucicaulting' the script. 'The whole play,' he says, 'was thickly sugared with spurious sentiment.'

Edith Mathews remembered the arrival in Belfast of the New York press comments on the production.

It was a Sunday night at Fred Morrow's house. Rutherford Mayne said, 'Oh, wait till you hear the reviews *The Drone* got,' and then he proceeded to read out the positively virulent criticisms. It was hopeless, it was footling, there wasn't a decent word to be said for it and anybody would be much better out in the street than wasting their time inside the theatre.[28]

Kane sent the author a cable asking what he should do in this crisis. A characteristic answer came back: 'Do nothing. A good play will outlive a failure. Time will tell.' Rutherford Mayne was right. It did. But Whitford Kane and John Campbell remained in New York, a serious loss to the Ulster Literary Theatre.

The perennial appearance of such favourites as *The Enthusiast* (1905) and *The Turn of the Road* (1906) might suggest that the U.L.T. worked on a limited repertory. This was not so. Every year saw one or two new plays staged by the company. Between 1904 and 1930 forty-eight plays were presented, most of them written by members of the Theatre. Of the forty-eight, about twenty were published, and of these a number are now unobtainable or to be found only in magazine files.

The most important, and prolific, dramatists of the U.L.T. were Rutherford Mayne with nine plays and Gerald Macnamara with eight. In 1909 Macnamara wrote *The Mist that Does Be on the Bog*, described by him as 'a fog in one act'. Mayne described it as 'an amusing parody on Synge's use of peasant speech in the *Playboy*, and its apt title has since passed into familiar currency.' This one-acter is really a farce in which the characters address each other in exchanges such as:

CLARENCE: And you think, kind ladies, that I have the gift of the bards upon me?
CISSIE: Sure it's as plain to be seen as the staff of a pike, for the beautiful words pour from your lips like a delf jug and it full of buttermilk.

The play was given its first production at the Abbey on 26–27 November 1909, and the parody seems to have been taken in good part. But, as John O'Leary has pointed out to me, fiom 1910 onward the U.L.T. staged the greater part of their Dublin seasons at the Gaiety Theatre.[29]

For its first season at the Belfast Opera House the U.L.T.

announced itself as 'in repertoire'. New writers were arising beside Mayne and Macnamara, even if some of their plays languished after a few nights and have since disappeared without trace. In 1911 and 1912 Miss M. F. Scott 'a native of Waterford, well-known in music and drama circles', wrote two curtain-raisers, *Charity* and *Family Rights*. More substantial was the contribution of William Paul who wrote three plays, *The Jerrybuilders* (1911), *Sweeping the Country* (1912), *The Tumulty Case* (1916). Little is known of Paul but reports suggest that he was a serious playwright. The four popular 'Ardkeel' farces, *The Skipper's Submarine* (1917), *The Lone Man* (1919), *Loaves and Fishes* (1921), *Missing Links* (1925), were the work of Charles K. Ayre (Charles Kerr). Kerr, a school-master, had been a prominent actor with the Theatre since 1909.

In 1911 Mayne gave the Theatre his one-act tragedy *Red Turf*, the brief telling of a murderous feud between Galway peasants over a turf bank. On 9 December 1912 the U.L.T. opened a week at the Opera House with *The Turn of the Road*, *Family Rights* and a new play by Macnamara, *Thompson in Tir-na-n'Og*. This one act fantasy, produced when the Home Rule agitation was at its height, was destined to become one of the most popular plays in the Theatre's repertoire. It tells the story of how Andy Thompson, engaged in the annual Sham Battle at Scarva, gets 'blew up' by the bursting of his old gun and wakes up, complete with Orange sash and bowler hat, in the Land of Eternal Youth among the heroes of Irish myth. They are not over-impressed by this sample of modern Ireland and depute the maiden, Grania, to wile his secrets from him:

GRANIA: And you know not if your army was victorious or not?

THOMPSON: Sure I told you I was on King William's side. Of course we won the day.

GRANIA: Why do you say 'of course'? The fortunes of war are so uncertain.

THOMPSON: Sure it wasn't a real fight. It was a sham fight.

GRANIA: A make-believe?

THOMPSON: Aye, the very thing.

GRANIA: But have you been in a real fight?

THOMPSON: O aye, I was in a scrap in Portadown last Sunday.

GRANIA: And whom were you fighting in Portadown?

THOMPSON: The Hibernians.

GRANIA: The Hibernians! But are not all the people in Eirinn Hibernians?

THOMPSON: Talk sense, woman dear.

GRANIA: Many changes must have come over Eirinn since the days of Cuchulain and Oisin. Then we were all Hibernians. I wish, dearest Thompson, that you were a Hibernian, too.

THOMPSON: You'll never see the day. And what's more I'll have nothing more to do with you, for I'm no believer in mixed marriages.

Gerald Morrow, Macnamara's nephew, says that *Thompson* 'was originally written by request for the Gaelic League. It was then in three acts. But they rejected it because they said "it held up the Gaelic heroes to ridicule". The author then made it into a one-act and gave it to the Ulster Theatre.' And for eighteen years it remained one of the U.L.T.'s most popular plays and was staged by the Theatre in Dublin, London, Liverpool and Cork. Stephen Gwynn writing of *Thompson* says that 'the shafts of mockery went home in different directions ... there was nothing at which the whole house did not laugh most heartily.'[30] Recalling how she first met Rutherford Mayne at the Abbey in 1927, Lady Gregory says that Mayne told her that 'the Ulster Theatre languishes, blames the Opera House in Belfast which turns down all new plays and falls back on *Thompson in Tir-na-n' Og*'[31] (On the other hand Rutherford Mayne's recollection is that it was the management's pre-dilection for the money-spinning *Drone* that brought about this lack of progress, an opinion shared by R. H. McCandless who recalls that Mayne's comedy was staged on three or four evenings during the U.L.T.'s short season, to the neglect of the work of new writers.)

The pairing of *Thompson* and *The Drone* in the Theatre's programme achieved not only a happy balance in length and variety but also had a remarkable effect on audiences in those days of political unrest. Rutherford Mayne remembers that on one occasion

> when there was a full house for the two plays with long queues for the 'gods', Mr McCann, who was the manager of the Opera House, came round and asked us not to let off too strong in *Thompson* because he had been informed that there were men up there who had been told that this play made fun of a certain Order, and that they were all lined up with rivets and bolts in their pockets. But we started off with *The Drone* and they got into really good humour with the result that when *Thompson* came on, instead of bolts and nuts and so forth landing on the stage, I never heard a play receive such acclamation at the end.[32]

Nothing could be farther removed from rural comedy or political burlesque than a piece contributed by Helen Waddell to the Theatre in 1915. The esoteric symbolism of *The Spoiled Buddha*,[33] an oriental legend, seems to have been over the heads of the audience and of the players. Edith Matthews, who saw the first production at the Opera House, remembers that 'the setting was very artistic and beautiful and the costumes were good and the acting was fearfully bad.' Gerald Macnamara upset the critics by playing the part of Binzura, the lighthearted disciple, with a brogue. Rutherford Mayne, the author's brother, 'brought great dignity to the part of the Buddha'. Shan F. Bullock, the Fermanagh novelist, who also contributed to the 1915 season, was, like Helen Waddell, better known for his non-dramatic writings. He turned his novel *The Squireen* into a three-act play *Snowdrop Jane*. It was not a success. Neither of these plays was revived by the Theatre.

On 2 February 1915 the Press announced that the official title of the company was now the Ulster Theatre. Gerald Macnamara is reported as saying that in '1904 the Theatre was composed of very young men with very mature ideas on literature. Ten years later these young men became modest and blacked out "Literary". [34]

Three seasons later, in 1918, the name of a new playwright appeared on the Theatre programmes. For their November season at the Opera House that year the U.T. produced *Away From the Moss* by George Moishiel, later famous as George Shiels, a dramatist of the first rank who was to reach his full stature with the Abbey Theatre and whose work, years later, was to contribute so greatly to the fame of the Ulster Group Theatre. Shiels gave the Ulster Theatre two other plays, *Felix Reid and Bob* (1919), and in 1930, *Cartney and Kevney*, first produced at the Abbey in 1927. In March 1918 the U.T. had produced *The Summons* by Leslie Lynd (Leslie Montgomery). The work of this writer was well known to the Ulster company, for in 1913 under the pseudonym of Lynn Doyle he had given them *Love and Land*, a comedy that almost rivalled *The Drone* in popularity. He contributed two more plays to the Theatre,

The Lilac Ribbon (1919), and *The Turncoats* (1922). Leslie Montgomery served as a bank official in various parts of the country and from the vantage point of this secular confession observed the comings and goings of his rural neighbours. *Ballygullion*, published in 1908, the first of numerous volumes of his short stories, was, as Stephen Gwynn says, 'read and laughed over through all Ireland'. If, unlike some of his contemporaries in the U.T., Doyle preferred the genial to the satirical, he was a conscientious artist and only Rutherford Mayne rivalled him in the art of the rural comedy. In December 1924 the U.T. produced St John Ervine's *The Ship* at the Gaiety Theatre, Dublin, and at the Opera House, Belfast. This play, it seems, was not revived by the Theatre.

Mayne and Macnamara were still to contribute substantially to the U.T. Between 1910 and 1923 the company presented six new works by Mayne: *The Captain of the Hosts* (1910) 'a full-length tragedy of Belfast city life' which was re-written as *Neil Gallina* and produced again in 1916; *If* (1914), a political farce; *Evening* (1913–4), a one-act playlet set in Co. Down; *Industry* (1917), 'the unsuccessful attempt of an Irish-American hustler to introduce big business into the sleepy town of Tubber-murry'; *Phantoms* (1923), a one-act fantasy. This was his last written work for the Ulster Theatre although it is probable that on occasions he travelled from Dublin to act for the company.

Rutherford Mayne was the most adventurous, the most prolific and the most successful dramatist of the Ulster Theatre and his work demands critical appraisal beyond the range of this history. In language and construction his plays are superior to almost all the writings of his contemporaries. *The Drone* takes pride of place. To its audiences the lure of the play has always been the irrepressible belief it reveals in the goodness of human nature. That this quality should be lodged in the character and expressed in the idiom of the East-Ulster Protestant made it, of course, all the more acceptable. Mayne was to write two plays for the Abbey Theatre, *Peter* (1930), and in 1934 *Bridgehead*, a play that James Bridie was to describe as '. . . a noble piece of work; stirring to the imagination and uplifting to the heart. It is a credit to the theatre and mankind'.

Following the plays already mentioned, Gerald Macnamara contributed *The Throwbacks* (1917), *Sincerity* (1918), *Fee, Faw, Fum* (1923), *No Surrender* (1928), *Who Fears to Speak* (1929), *Thompson on Terra Firma* (1935). It is melancholy but true that Macnamara, who as playwright and actor delighted audiences for thirty years, is not noticed in any literary history; and that of eight plays, only one, *Thompson in Tir-na-n'Og*, second in popularity to *The Drone*, was ever published in book form.[35]

In so far as Gerald Macnamara has come down to posterity as a laughter-maker first and foremost, his genius has been unfairly diminished. Behind his writings is discernible a serious and informed political intelligence familiar with the intricacies and paradoxes of whatever period of Irish history he has chosen as a backcloth to his satire. Indeed it is this exhaustive knowledge that kept his pilloried audiences suspended in a state of bewilderment and laughter. He knew their sacred cows by name better than they themselves did. David Kennedy has said that the pedigree of *Thompson in Tir-na-n'Og* 'was by Henrik Ibsen out of Cathleen Ni Houlihan'.

Of the alternatives offered by A. E. Malone to Irish writers, 'either to improve the community of which they are a part, or . . . to wound their neighbours by laughing at them,' Macnamara leaned strongly towards the former. The more intelligent of his contemporaries saw his plays as trenchant if entertaining political comment. When *Thompson* was produced at the Scala Theatre, London in 1923, the critic of the *Daily*

Dispatch wrote: 'This play is really propaganda in the form of serio-comedy. It is directed, primarily, against the false kind of Ulsteria born of fanatical ignorance, which has done so much to discredit the real sentiment and patriotism of the North. Lord Birkenhead, I believe, was amongst the audience. No doubt he found the performance instructive.'

The first production at the Gaiety Theatre of the three-act fantasy *The Throwbacks* drew from a Dublin critic an illuminating comment on Macnamara's qualities of audacity and invention.

The satirist in Ireland treads no primrose path, more especially if, like the author of *The Throwbacks*, his shafts are winged at all parties. Where others who have tried the same course move as gingerly as a ship in a mine-field, Mr Macnamara drives riotously ahead, with a gale of laughter from his victims filling the sails of his craft.

It is not that he deals half-hearted blows. Few of his fellows wield a sharper sword or can drive home such deadly thrusts. But there is never malice in his wit, and, above all—and we imagine this enables him to take risks that with anybody else would provoke a riot—he never lectures his audience from Olympian heights. If Mr Macnamara has a fault it is that he stuffs his play too full of good things. It is really a defect in *The Throwbacks* that it has not a dull moment, and he ought in justice to his audience remember that one cannot laugh continuously through three acts. It sounds strange advice to give to a writer of comedy, but one would seriously counsel Mr Macnamara not to be afraid of being a little dull occasionally.[36]

Rutherford Mayne wrote of him: 'He hated cruelty in any shape or form—or lack of thought for things beautiful; the cruelty of extremists who hammered on dogmas, or on drums, or on human beings is mercilessly satirised in all his plays.' He is entitled to recognition 'as one of the finest comic geniuses that the Irish dramatic revival has produced.'

It is possible to make an arbitrary division of the Ulster Theatre's story into three phases: from 1904 to 1911, the years of promise; from 1912 to 1920, the years of fruition; from 1920 to 1934, the years of slow but perceptible decay. Various seasons have been advanced to explain the decline that set in around 1920. Gerald Morrow has said: 'The ten years from 1924 to 1934 were the most difficult of the Theatre's existence and also the most uninteresting. Although fifteen new productions took place in the ten years there was none of outstanding merit and few, if any, could be revived again at the Opera House.' In 1920 the Theatre played for one week only, and that in Dublin, the shortest season since 1912. Again in 1925 and in 1926 there were no productions in Belfast, and in 1927 no Ulster Theatre season anywhere. 1934 was the Ulster Theatre's last year at the Opera House. In that season the Theatre and the Opera House lost money on *The Schemer* by Thomas Kelly and *A Majority of One* by William Liddell. Thereafter the company was refused the stage they had filled with such distinction for twenty-six years.

Time and the frenetic politics of the period wrought changes in the society. 'The years of the First World War and the 1916 Rising,' says David Kennedy, 'had been years of sorrow for many of the members for one cause or another. Then the post-war troubles in Belfast, with the hardening of political feeling seemed to have ended the old happy days.' Bulmer Hobson and Joseph Campbell had long ago been drawn into political activity. John Campbell and Lewis Purcell had emigrated. Rutherford Mayne and Lynn Doyle had gone to live in the South. Of the significant playwrights of the U.L.T. only Gerald Macnamara remained in Ulster. Yet, notwithstanding what had happened in the intervening years, there were still those with the Theatre who remembered that it had been fathered by political opinion, the affirmative response of a group of young Protestants to the challenge of nationalism and the Irish Literary Revival.

The Ulster Theatre remained an amateur organisation until the end. In 1940 it came under the guidance of Gerald Morrow, a nephew of Gerald Macnamara. An opportunity arose to merge the U.T. as a constituent part into a new drama organisation formed by a number of actors and producers who wished to see a professional theatre in Ulster. After a trial period Gerald Morrow withdrew from the scheme, commenting later: 'Away back in my mind I remembered that in 1904 the Ulster Literary Theatre had declared that it sought before the comfortable things of the body the more comfortable things of the spirit.' As the new organisation became the Ulster Group Theatre he was possibly rather precipitate in his decision.

Nevertheless Morrow was correct in detecting a shift in the aims of those who had come into the company in its later years. One of those who wanted to see the Ulster Theatre put on a commercial footing was H. Richard Hayward who, with Abram Rish, had contributed a one-act farce, *The Jew's Fiddle* (1920) and his own burlesque melodrama, *Huge Love* (1924), to the Theatre's presentations. In 1930 there was a policy dispute over the issue. The details are vague, except that it resulted in Rutherford Mayne resigning from the Theatre committee although he appeared in a number of productions after this date. Dr Padraig Gregory, one of the earliest members of the U.L.T. recalled: 'There were certain elements who got into the Theatre . . . and they got the taste for money and they were not content as we were to save our money up with a view to acquiring a theatre.'[37]

But the Ulster Theatre never acquired a home. In St John Ervine's opinion it 'suffered severely from the fact that it was a society for *occasional* productions and that it had no theatre of its own.'[38] Rutherford Mayne puts it down to lack of funds:

I remember distinctly going with Jack and Fred Morrow and Lewis Purcell up street after street looking for some vacant place in which we could get a theatre. Eventually we found one, an old disused stable, but the rent demanded was beyond us. Nobody in the Ulster Theatre had any money worth talking about ... except Lewis Purcell who had independent means. A public appeal for funds was launched and one gentleman sent a subscription of five shillings, only one out of the entire population of Belfast.[39]

A number of people thought that the Northern Ireland Government should have followed the example of the South and granted a theatre subsidy. 'It would be surely criminal,' wrote Whitford Kane in 1931, 'to allow any theatre with such a fine record as the U.L.T. to sink into oblivion, but, if neglected much longer, this may be expected. Subsidising the Ulster Theatre would win for Ulster a position in the world of literature and art.'[40] George Shiels, from the viewpoint of the dramatist, said: 'Belfast needs a little theatre with a corporate existence, a home of its own and a subsidy. Such a one would do much for the cultural life of the city and would attract the services of writers who devote the major part of their time to writing ... It would be able to accept plays for their artistic merit alone without thought of the box-office receipts.'[41]

Those idealistic young men and women who came together at the beginning of the century, playwrights, actors, stage directors, may have failed to build the fabric of a playhouse. They did better. They raised a tradition of living theatre in Ulster that the demolition men can never pull down.

3

Theatre in the Thirties

A century's span of melodrama and music fell in rubble when, in 1961, the Empire Theatre in Belfast was pulled down. On this site in Victoria Square in the 1860s stood the Imperial Colosseum Music Hall. In turn Travers' Musical Lounge and The Buffalo, it appeared in 1894 in gilt, plush and crimson as the Belfast Empire Theatre of Varieties. From theatrical lodgings in nearby Joy Street came all the 'truly great, original and only'; Little Tich, Gertie Gitana, Marie Lloyd, G. H. Elliott, Harry Lauder, and (it is said) Charles Chaplin to tread its boards. And Ireland's darlings, Talbot O'Farrell, Jimmy O'Dea and Belfast's own Willie John Ashcroft, each in his hey-day and night. But other voices, more to our purpose, were heard in the Empire Theatre. 'It was here,' wrote Louis Gilbert, student of Belfast's theatres and music halls, 'that I heard my first Ulster play; the Limavady Players' production of Shiels's *Professor Tim*. For years the Rosario Players with Lorenzo Martin in *The Auction at Killybuck* was an annual treat for me.'[1]

In the thirties the Empire was the home of the Empire Players or Belfast Repertory Theatre Company. Founded in

1929 by Richard Hayward with Gerald Morrison manager of the Empire as co-director and J. R. Mageean as producer, they aspired to be to Belfast what the Abbey Theatre was to Dublin. They are probably best remembered as the company or at least the nucleus of players who, with the Irish-American director Donovan Pedelty, made two popular feature films, *The Luck of the Irish* and *Irish and Proud of It*. They were a highly-skilled company and for about eight years filled the gap left by the declining Ulster Theatre.

Actors who appeared with the Belfast Repertory were Richard Hayward, Charles Fagan, Kitty Murphy, Jack Gavin, Charlotte Tedlie, Mimi Mageean, R. H. McCandless, Kathleen Porter, Elizabeth Begley, Nan Cullen, Dan Fitzpatrick, Robert Forsythe Boyd, Terence Grainger, Rodney Malcolmson, Elma Hayward, Norah Nairn, Gerry Morrow and, of course, Jimmy Mageean, one of the finest comic actors on the Irish stage. Many of them had appeared with the old Ulster Theatre and were to carry on to the Ulster Group Theatre.

With any Ulster company of any durability are associated the names of two or three playwrights. The Belfast Repertory Company was no exception. At the Abbey Theatre on 13 October 1932 they presented *Workers*, the first play by a Belfast dramatist, Tom Carnduff. Its success in Dublin seems to have been due, at least in part, to the author's ability to set before the audience a group of Belfast shipyard workers 'hard-drinking, hard-swearing, hard-up', all of them struggling to keep out of the dole queue. From the stage Carnduff told his highly appreciative audience that 'for a Belfast working-man like myself, to have shown in a theatre with the tradition of the Abbey some of the heroism and the humanity of the men whom I have worked with all my life, is a great thing. Tonight you have lifted one of the workers of Belfast a little higher than he

5

has ever been before.' The *Irish Times* critic said: 'Judged by the severe standards of the Abbey, this play is not a good one, but for an out-of-work shipyard employee, who has had no previous experience of the stage, it is rather a remarkable achievement.'[2] On the quality of Carnduff's dialogue several critics invoked the name of O'Casey.

Carnduff's second contribution to the B.R.T., *Machinery*, a 'Belfast Factory Play in four acts,' opened at the Abbey Theatre on 6 March 1933. Again his work was faulted because of its poor construction, and praised for the vitality of its dialogue. One Dublin critic wrote:

> The success of *Machinery* is a signal instance of the triumph of natural ability over technical inefficiency. It is a remarkable play, the author has a mind like a camera; he takes the life of the Belfast industrial worker and reproduces it on the stage with the accuracy, and almost the artlessness, of a statistical table. He has other good qualities. He has an excellent sense of the dramatic, a sound appreciation of character, and ability to write terse, vivid, powerful dialogue that is photographic of his Belfast industrial workers.[3]

In the opinion of a critic: 'Richard Hayward's company presented the play very ably. The staging of the mechanic's shop achieved more realism than we are accustomed to at the Abbey Theatre . . . '[4]

For his third play, *Traitors*, Carnduff took his characters from the Belfast back-streets. It had its première on 22 January 1934 at the Empire Theatre, Belfast, and the critics agreed that it showed a marked advance in the playwright's stagecraft. That first night audience, according to the *Irish News*, was 'treated to a drama of almost stark realism, characters . . . with the natural virtues and failings of their type. The play deals with people who to satisfy a jealous motive play traitor to their class and give information against a neighbour who has been falsely obtaining unemployment benefit . . . Mr Carnduff's third play is undoubtedly an advance both in technique and dramatic quality over his previous efforts.'[5]

Before he turned to the theatre, Tom Carnduff had published two volumes of verse, *Songs from the Shipyards* (1924) and *Songs of an Out-of-Work* (1932). Yet, unlike his contemporary, Hugh Quinn, who managed to infuse some lyricism into that most intractable of material, Belfast speech, Carnduff's dialogue was noted for its prosaic 'naturalism'. Possibly because he tired of this timbre, Carnduff went back to the revolutionary period of 1798 for his fourth and last play. It was, he says in his unpublished autobiography, 'my supreme effort at playwriting'.

Castlereagh opened at the Empire Theatre on 21 January 1935, with Richard Hayward in the title role. The play 'admirably acted, costumed and staged' was highly successful. Hayward as Castlereagh, Harold Goldblatt as Alexander Knox and R. H. McCandless as Jamie Hope were commended by the critics. The playwright made little effort to dissemble his sympathies; the Chief Secretary was 'Bloody Castlereagh', an appellation cordially accepted by a large part of the audience. I can recall Hayward throwing open a lattice and with a wave of his hand to the scenic backcloth crying: 'They lie who say I do not love this country!'—a declaration which we in the Gods received in silence broken by a storm of jeers, groans and orange peel. The play contains some remarkable confrontations: Hope and Knox at the revolutionists' Muddlers Club, and particularly Castlereagh and the Rev. James Porter at Mount Stewart. H. Montgomery Hyde, the biographer and historian whose *Rise of Castlereagh* had appeared in 1933, contributed an article to the Press in which he enumerated the historical implausibilities in the play. To this Carnduff replied, claiming reasonably enough, that 'a dramatist does not write history; he makes use of it for the purpose of revealing the characteristics of the subject he wishes to portray.'[6] Montgomery Hyde was generous in his criticism: 'he (Carnduff) has written a remarkably fine play, which deserves to be seen; those concerned in its production and performance are to be congratulated.'

Carnduff's work is in danger of being forgotten, undeservedly. Changed social conditions may have robbed his plays of some of their conflict; no doubt, too, there were faults in their construction; but the evidence of the Dublin and Belfast critics testify to the vigour and effectiveness of his dramatic writing. And if ever a man knew of what he was writing, it was Tom Carnduff. Recalling his hopes and fears on that first night of his first play at the Abbey he said: 'Not that failure could mean any material change in my life, for there is no stage below labouring for a livelihood—except starvation.'

In 1936 the Belfast Repertory Theatre presented another new Ulster play, *The Early Bird*, by James Douglas of Coleraine, whose four-act comedy opened at the Empire Theatre on 20 January. The *Northern Whig* recognised in it 'all the elements of Ulster comedy such as we have known for many years now.' On their 1937 visit to Dublin the company took with them two one-act plays by Hugh Quinn, *Collecting the Rent* and *A Quiet Twelfth*[7], which had their first airing in the Gaiety Theatre on 6–7 December as curtain-raisers to *Love and Land* and *Traitors*. Shortly after this the B.R.T. was wound up but a few years later members of the company were to work together again in the Ulster Group Theatre.

It is impossible in this survey to give the amateur movement in Ulster the consideration it deserves. At one end there are groups still working at pieces that one thought were forgotten long ago, at the other there are societies presenting with professional finesse plays from contemporary world theatre. Perhaps this is misleading in that it suggests an inflexibility and unchangeableness in all the parts of an activity that runs from Omagh to Bangor and from Coleraine to Newry. The facts are different: amateur societies at widely separated localities and periods have risen, flourished for a time and subsided, each of them contributing a passage, great or small, to the history of the theatre in Ulster.

One of the most influential of these societies was the Northern Drama League which came into existence largely through the efforts of W. R. Gordon, an early member of the U.L.T., Richmond Noble and H. O. Meredith, Professor of Economics at the Queen's University, Belfast, with Lucy Gaffikin as secretary. The University Dramatic Society was associated with the new organisation and then withdrew after a season, but R. M. Henry, Professor of History, as President of the League, and H. O. Meredith as author, translator and producer, maintained a link between the University and the company for many years. In October 1923 the *Northern Whig* informed its readers:

> The Northern Drama League, which owes its inception to articles and correspondence in this paper, begins its activities proper this month. Its object is to promote the amateur performances of such good plays as are unlikely to be produced in the theatres of the city ... The provisional programme includes Euripides, Massinger, Molière, Dryden, Ibsen, Yeats's *Deirdre* and Shaw's *Androcles and the Lion*. The success of the venture will be followed with interest by a wide circle of friends.

Questioning whether or not the plays of Euripides or Ibsen could ever hope to have as wide an appeal as *The Drone*, the writer warned the new society of the dangers of an over-ambitious programme.[8]

Undeterred, the N.D.L. pursued its objective of bringing good theatre to Belfast, adding among others the names of Racine, Lessing, Vanbrugh and Strindberg to its play library. New plays produced by the League were *Apollo in Mourne* by Richard Rowley, Christie Gilbert's *The Stocking*, Ralph Meredith's *Peter Pedagogue* and *First Samuel* by Graeme Roberts. An interesting presentation was H. O. Meredith's *Andree McKée*, 'an extravaganza of England in 1945 based upon the *Andromaque* of Racine'. One critic said that these plays 'would in themselves justify the existence of the N.D.L.' Many of the names that appear in the sixteen years of the League's existence became well-known in subsequent Belfast companies. But as producer, Margaret C. Weir, told me: 'There was no star system in the League. If you played lead in one production as like as not you swept the dressing-rooms for the next.'

In founding the competitive Northern Dramatic Feis the N.D.L. greatly benefited the amateur theatre movement in Ulster. Later, these annual drama contests, adjudicated by well-known theatre personalities, were organised by the Association of Ulster Amateur Dramatic Societies (they also published a lively theatre journal, *The Script*). The task of organising is now in the capable hands of the Association of Ulster Drama Festivals. Staged at first in the Empire Theatre, the Feis moved, in later years, to the Grand Opera House. Among the societies appearing in the 1936 Feis at the Opera House were the 'Bangor Unemployed Men', a reminder of the widespread and terrible unemployment in Ulster in the thirties. I like to think that their appearance was due to the efforts of Professor Meredith to bring organised theatre to the workless men and women in the city.

Since its opening in 1895 by the Shakespearean actor, Sir Frank Benson, the Grand Opera House has been the principal theatre in Belfast. In its seventy years the illustrious from Sarah Bernhardt to Sara Allgood have entered its stage door in Glengall Street. Grand Opera Houses are not usually expected to house resident theatrical companies. But in 1939 a number of cross-channel actors and actresses stranded in Dublin on the outbreak of war came north to the Opera House, dubbed themselves the Savoy Players, and six nights a week for six years entertained Belfast audiences and many thousands of service men and women stationed in Northern Ireland. The demands of the times brought changes in the company but theatre-goers of an older generation will remember with pleasure Evelyn Keery, Norman Chidgey, June Daunt, Basil Lord, Guy Rolfe, Jane Aird, Sheila Manahan, Malachi Keegan and two talented young Belfast actresses, Jean Hamilton and Patricia Stewart. Many tributes were paid to the Savoy Players during those years of war. When the company presented its two hundredth play an American journalist wrote: 'These players are firmly a part of Belfast, so thoroughly a part of the entertainment life of the city that they are known and loved by thousands of servicemen of all the Allied Nations. Few members of the entertainment world are doing more than they are doing right here. I have seen many plays in London, Los Angeles, New York. In no city or theatre have I seen players so warmly received, night after night, week after week.'

4

The Ulster Group Theatre

In May 1905 when the Ulster Literary Theatre was presenting, amid critical acclaim, *The Enthusiast* and *The Little Cowherd*, a young actor, R. H. McCandless, destined to become one of the outstanding figures of the Irish stage, was appearing with a company called the 'Ulster Dramatic Society' in a melodrama, *Still Waters Run Deep*. I mention this to dispel the notion that the theatres discussed in this book came to life suddenly, inexplicably and alone. On the contrary, there have always been excellent dramatic societies, contemporaneous with whichever was the leading Theatre of the time, active not only in Belfast but in provincial centres such as Newry, Omagh, Limavady, Londonderry, Coleraine and Bangor. Indeed the tradition of theatre in Ulster, slender but ever-renascent, has been kept alive not by managements or patrons and most certainly not by civic authorities, but rather by small groups of actors, usually young, often penniless, always, theatrically speaking, homeless.

In the winter of 1939–40 three such companies went to the making of the Ulster Group Theatre: the Ulster Theatre at this time under the guidance of Gerald Morrow and Nita Hardie, the Jewish Institute Dramatic Society led by their producer, Harold Goldblatt, and the Northern Irish Players. The N.I.P., the strongest of the three, was itself a recently-formed amalgam of prominent actors drawn from various amateur companies such as the St John's Dramatic Society of Belfast, the Stella Maris Players and the Carrickfergus Players.

The documentary material on the origin and development of the Ulster Group Theatre is of the scantiest. The bundle of plays that I was able to secure, ranging over ten years and more, proved to be incomplete and undated. For this chapter, therefore, I have drawn largely on the reminiscences of early members which were recorded for a B.B.C. documentary programme[1] on the Theatre broadcast in 1965. Where the source of a statement is not given it is taken from this programme. There are gaps in the story and, understandably, times when the accounts do not match. But it is the fullest record of a theatre company which, unlike the U.L.T., seems to have had little interest in noting its day-to-day history.

It is possible to detect in the vigorous amateur dramatic movement of the late thirties a definite move towards some form of professionalism. This was encouraged, no doubt, by two interesting attempts to found a professional company in Belfast, the Little Theatre (1933–6) and The Playhouse (1937), both housed in the Ulster Minor Hall. Rutherford Mayne could well say that 'the Ulster Theatre died as it lived—in penury.' Here necessity could have been mistaken for a virtue. But the young actors of 1937 thought they could tell the difference between commercialism and professionalism. One of them was J. A. Fitzsimons, now a school principal in County Down. His answer on this point can be taken as representing the opinion of thirty years ago. 'When you say it was my intention to introduce professionalism—yes, certainly, the standard of professionalism, rather than . . . in the accepted sense of having a financial return from it.'

This is not so far from the aim of the U.L.T. James Fitzsimons explains what he means by introducing the 'standard of professionalism.' 'About 1937,' he says 'after playing with amateur groups in Belfast I realised that we weren't getting very far—there was always this shortage of props and costumes and we could never accumulate money to dress our stages properly and . . . we weren't learning an awful lot about the art of play production.' He discovered that there were other actors equally concerned about the lack of policy and purpose inseparable from an amateur theatre made up of a dozen or so small societies each 'doing its best'. Among the actors and producers were Elizabeth Begley, John McDade, James R. Mageean, James Connolly, Joseph Tomelty, Ann Breene and John F. Tyrone. Elizabeth Begley remembers a meeting at her home in the autumn of 1938, '. . . when we talked over the forming of a company. We had each belonged to different dramatic societies and we though it would be a good idea to get together.'

The aim of these discussions was, according to Fitzsimons, to form 'a semi-professional society wherein about 60 per cent of the profits would be ploughed back into the society and the remainder distributed among the players.' And he adds: 'the policy of distributing the profits among the players had an edge to it in so far as it would mean that the players would be personally and collectively responsible for any losses occurring in our productions.' For their first presentation the new company (under the name of the Ulster Repertory Company) staged Louis Walsh's *Auction at Killybuck* at St Mary's Hall on Boxing Night, 1938.

As an outlet for their talent and energy, the new association, renamed the Northern Irish Players, was enthusiastically supported by the actors and producers invited to join it. The original members are given as: Elizabeth Begley, Ann Boreen, Nan Cullen, Bee Duffell, Dan Fitzpatrick, James Fitzsimons, Lydia Gallagher, John McDade, J. R. Mageean, R. H. McCandless, James Connolly, Charles Owens, Jack O'Malley, John F. Tyrone and Joseph Tomelty. The producer, J. R. Mageean; stage manager, Dan Fitzpatrick; wardrobe mistress, Nan Cullen; secretary, Lydia Gallagher; librarian, Ann Boreen. For professional reasons John Moss adopted the stage name 'John F. Tyrone'; 'Ann Boreen' was a light disguise for Ann Breene, and later James Boyce, at that time a schoolmaster, took the name 'Seamus Ussher'. By the mid-thirties the majority of actors worked under their own names—an interesting comment on the change that had taken place in public opinion since the early days of the U.L.T.

The aims of the N.I.P., printed in their first programme were:

> ... that this Company is to produce plays by local and other Irish authors, as well as plays of the English and Continental stage. Its ultimate aim is to foster and develop a permanent home for drama in Belfast. It is felt that with the wealth of acting talent in the Province and with the support and patronage of the playgoing public this is well within the bounds of accomplishment.

The second company contributing to the U.G.T. was the Ulster Theatre, managed by Gerald Morrow and Bill and Nita Hardie. When they had lived at Oldham the Hardies contributed much to the success of one of the leading North of England amateur companies, the Curtain Theatre, Rochdale, where Bill had been dramatic director and Nita had produced and acted. Among the prominent members of the Ulster

Theatre at this time were Harold Simpson, Stella Davies, Arthur Ross, Mary Morrison, Lucy Young, Jean Woods, Allan McClelland, Jack McQuoid, Harry S. Gibson, Pat Agnew and Muriel North.

The Jewish Institute Dramatic Society first came into prominence at the 1929 Northern Drama Festival when the adjudicator, Frank Fay, awarded the premier award, the President's Cup, to the company for their production of Israel Zangwill's *The Melting Pot*. A highly successful company, they presented over the years works by Chekhov, Rice, Maugham, Shaw and Ibsen. Among the Jewish Players who came into the U.G.T. were Beatrice Hurwitz, Izzy Samuels, Victor Hurwitz, Bernard Barnett, Sonney Hodes and Solly Glover who also worked for the Ulster Theatre. (From play programmes it is evident that even before the formation of the U.G.T. there was a considerable borrowing and lending of actors among the leading dramatic societies.)

The idea of a 'group' company was considered in the autumn of 1939. 'About then', says James R. Mageean, 'Harold Goldblatt asked me to join him, with the Ulster Theatre, in an attempt to form a permanent professional theatre. I said "yes", if the Northern Ireland Players would agree to do so. They did so, and we joined the other two companies, hence the name "Group Theatre," and set to work.' The new society had to set to work to find a stage. For over thirty years the Ulster Minor Hall had been the home of a number of companies. It was indifferently proofed against the sounds of excitable and clamorous events held in the main hall, and the actors often had to compete against the noise of revivalist meetings, dance sessions and boxing matches.

Back in 1933 the Minor Hall had been occupied by the Little Theatre, a professional repertory company led by

L. Griffith-Knight and N. O'D. Grimshaw. Among the plays presented was *The Mills of God*, by the Ulster playwright, Harry S. Gibson. But the menu offered was made up very largely of West End successes. For three years this company staged many admirable performances for the Ulster playgoer. In May 1937 the name was changed to the Playhouse, under the management of Harald Norway.

In an attempt to regain audiences for Ulster plays the management of the Playhouse sought the help of an Honorary Provisional Advisory Board, the members of which were Richard Hayward, David Kennedy, J. R. Mageean, R. H. McCandless and Gerald Morrow. The programmes announced that 'the Playhouse doors are open to all Ulster play producing societies, and their plays and players will be welcomed by both the Playhouse management and players, and every help and assistance will be rendered to visitors whenever they occupy the Playhouse stage.' In the first month of the new company's life Richard Hayward announced that 'the Advisory Committee had already compiled a list of 23 Ulster plays and (that) next week Jack Loudan's *The Ball Turns Once* would be presented.'[2] Loudan's play, which had been produced at the Abbey Theatre and in New York by Whitford Kane, brought back to the Belfast stage Kitty Murphy and Marion Crimmons, two names well-known to an earlier generation of theatre-goers. But the scheme to present Ulster plays had little effect on the box-office and the Playhouse, for all its forward-looking policy, had to ring down the curtain.

On the week commencing 12 June 1939 the Northern Irish Players presented two plays at the Belfast Empire Theatre, Maugham's *The Letter* and Joseph Tomelty's *Barnum Was Right* (originally titled *The Beauty Competition*). The actors' names are not set out against the stage characters but listed together at the bottom of the playbill and already one can see a fusion among prominent members from various societies. The Northern Irish Players for this short season at the Empire Theatre were Lily Begley, Victor Hurwitz, James Connolly, Irene McArdle, George Allport, Valerie Holmes, Nan Cullen, John McDade, Joseph Tomelty, Beatrice Hurwitz, Lucy Young, Bee Duffell, Jack McQuoid, Dan Fitzpatrick, Jack O'Malley, James Fitzsimons and Charles Owens; the producers were Harold Goldblatt and James Mageean.

The Empire Theatre venture, according to John F. Tyrone who was secretary-manager of the N.I.P., showed a financial loss. If the new organisation was to have a future a smaller permanent home had to be found. Although he was aware that there had been two recent theatrical failures there, Harold Goldblatt recommended the renting of the Ulster Minor Hall. But, as he discovered, the Belfast Corporation, owners of the Ulster Hall, were well aware of the transitory nature of professional theatricals. ' "I would like to take this place," he informed the officials at the City Hall. The rent was six pounds a week, which wasn't too much. But the Superintendent of the Estates Department said, "No, no, no, we can't give it to you." I said "But I'm prepared to give you security." "No", said he, "You're bound to fail." And the only way I could get it was by paying three months' rent in advance. But there we had the lease.'

It would be misleading to suggest that the people who founded the Ulster Group Theatre believed that extra attention to production and the pay-box would, somehow, change their company into a 'professional' theatre. In fact, there was already a considerable amount of professional experience in this amalgam of players. J. R. Mageean had been for some years with the Sir Frank Benson Shakespeare Company; R. H.

McCandless appeared in Belfast theatres with such actors as Godfrey Tearle and Matheson Lang and could have accompanied them further afield; Harold Goldblatt and others had worked with L. Griffith-Knight and the Playhouse company. And there were still actors about who had been touched by the magic of Fred Morrow.

Although they had banded under the title of the U.G.T., each of the three constituent companies retained its separate identity. The Theatre opened its twelve-week experimental period on 11 March 1940, when, as the programme states, the 'Group Theatre presents an Ulster Theatre production'. This was the Bridie/Frank comedy *Storm in a Teacup*, produced by Nita Hardie with settings by George Morrow. The Press greeted the new Theatre and its first presentation with enthusiasm. 'Control and management,' reported one paper, 'are in the hands of men who have their roots in Ulster, and it will be their aim to develop native talent among players and authors too. It is a brave venture in times like these, and one that deserves to be supported.' Writing of the play the critic commented: 'It was fitting that Nita Hardie, who produced it, should carry off the chief honours as Mrs Flannigan in a performance that would stand comparison with Sara Allgood herself. First rate, too, were Stella Davis, a charming talented young actress, as Mrs Thompson, and Muriel North, who as Mrs Skirving, delivered her lines with point and spirit.' The report concluded with the news that 'next week Mr Goldblatt's company will be seen in *French Leave* and the week following the Northern Irish Players will make their bow in *Barnum Was Right*. A fine start and a happy prospect for all who value the living theatre.'

It *was* a fine start and in the twelve weeks each of the three companies presented four plays, plays ranging from *The*

Chinese Bungalow to Hugh Quinn's *Mrs McConaghy's Money*. 'At the end of those three months,' Harold Goldblatt says, 'we had made about £40 profit. This had never been heard of before, so we decided to carry on. But we had no policy, we were floundering in the dark.'

There was, in fact, a break at this period in the Theatre's activities. The programme for the twelfth and final production informed the audience that

> ... the production of *John Ferguson* brings to an end the first and experimental season which opened three months ago, and which, in spite of tremendous difficulties, has proved to be a striking success in every way. It is intended, circumstances permitting, to re-open the Theatre in the Autumn, and with the experience gained during the past twelve weeks it is hoped that future productions will maintain, and even improve upon, the high standard which has been achieved

A play a week had proved extremely hard work for actors and producers and the very success of the enterprise dictated a pause for some rethinking about the Theatre's present and future. John F. Tyrone recalls that the profits from the box-office were quickly dealt with:

> At that time ... our artistes were getting the magnificent sum of 10s. 6d. a week. It wasn't in payment or any recognition of their ability, it was just to pay their expenses. We had a few pounds left over—something about £48, and we decided that we would divide this up and pay the players for the number of performances and so they got a little bonus, usually about a pound for each performance. And that ran away with the money. Then we had a meeting to decide whether to go on or not.

This pause in activities was brought about not so much by

indecision as the need for reorganisation. The Theatre, of course, had come to the end of its lease; the originators, somewhat to their surprise, had a success on their hands, a success that made the discovery of a policy a matter of immediate concern. There were a number of changes and shifts in the body theatrical, the only one worth noting here being the withdrawal of the Ulster Theatre from the Group organisation.

A number of the early members recall that this change coincided with the end of the Theatre's first run. But apparently the secession wasn't quite so abrupt. When the U.G.T. decided to continue and reopened at the Ulster Minor Hall on 2 September 1940, their first production was Maugham's *The Circle* produced by Nita Hardie, and in the cast were names associated with the Ulster Theatre, Harold Simpson, Eric Holmes, Constance Higginson and Rosemary Leeper Wilson. But from this date the titles of the three constituent companies disappeared and the programmes read 'The Ulster Group Theatre presents . . .' The Theatre became the property of a board of directors—R. H. McCandless, Harold Goldblatt, J. R. Mageean, John F. Tyrone, Joseph Tomelty, Jack O'Malley and Dan Fitzpatrick. The Manager was Charles Owens, Fitzpatrick was Stage Manager and Tyrone remained as secretary.

The play that followed, *Counsel's Opinion* by Gilbert Wakefield, is interesting in that the cast included Patrick Bogues of the Omagh Players, an actor and producer who has done inestimable work in keeping drama alive in the western part of the Province. Then, on 16 September 1940, came the play that was to guarantee the immediate solvency of the Group and contribute a large part to its eventual success as the Theatre of Ulster. 'Bob McCandless came to a meeting one morning', says Harold Goldblatt, 'and said "We should do Ervine's *Boyd's Shop*—it's a good play." We put on *Boyd's Shop* and it

6

was crowded. So we ran it for another week, we ran it for fifteen weeks. That really started us, gave us an insight as to what our policy should be. The major portion of our work was to be the Ulster Play.'

The run of *Boyd's Shop* was not continuous. It was taken off after a week. But some quality in St John Ervine's play reminded men and women of homely virtues reported missing if not already dead in those sombre early days and black nights of the War. The letters began to arrive at the Theatre. The public wanted to see and hear Andrew Boyd and his neighbours from Donaghreagh again. So on 25 November R. H. McCandless's production took the stage once more, and apart from a short break at the end of the year, filled the Theatre until the heavy air raid on the city on 14 April 1941. On the following evening John F. Tyrone arrived at the Theatre.

We were all ready to play, but when we got to the Theatre there were only a few of us there. The Carrickfergus actors, Jean Lundy, Elizabeth McKeown and R. H. hadn't turned up. And Jack O'Malley was missing. But before house opening time the Carrickfergus people arrived. How they got through to Belfast I don't know. And O'Malley, who'd been up all night as a firewatcher, came stumbling in, tin helmet and all, ready to play his part—you couldn't see him for dust and dirt. I'll never forget another strange thing about that evening. An old lady of over seventy years of age and her two daughters, arrived for the show. The police then told us that we couldn't open because there was an unexploded bomb at the back. So the show was off, much to the chagrin of the old lady. I need hardly add that there were no other audience there. That shut us up for quite a long time.

One of the reasons for the popularity of *Boyd's Shop* was the playing of the part of Andrew Boyd by Robert Dempster, originally of the Carrickfergus Players. Dempster, in R. H. McCandless's opinion, '... was a great find, a very conscientious actor, lovely voice, and never satisfied. He was very anxious to do the right thing. But he was a natural actor. Wild horses wouldn't have drawn him to play a part that he thought he was unfit for.' He also possessed, according to John F. Tyrone, a quality that not only enhanced his worth as an artist but was much appreciated by his fellow-actors. 'He was the type of artist,' says Tyrone, 'to whom you'd give a three-act play on Friday and tell him the first rehearsal was on Monday morning. When he came in he would hand the producer the book. He had it all off, not only his own part, but most of everybody else's. He had the most amazing memory, never forgot a line, and could take anybody else out without a prompter.'

The manner in which the Group Theatre was formed provided the company with a range of acting ability and experience that would have been difficult to bring together in any other way. The U.G.T. were able to present with congruity and often with distinction Ibsen, Sheridan, Chekhov, Pinero, Bridie, Odets, Cesare Viola, Maugham, Shaw, Priestley, Coward and Rattigan. But the inner impulse and indeed the outer and public claim was for the Ulster play. (The U.G.T. produced plays by Southern writers like Lennox Robinson, D'Alton, O'Casey, Behan and Walter Macken. But the plays of the Theatre's main dramatists, Shiels, Ervine, Tomelty and others, although also Irish, were accepted and appreciated by the public as Ulster in locale, atmosphere, idiom and dialect.)

Alfred Arnold, who had worked with the Cambridge University Footlights, and became associated with the Group Theatre in 1940, was of the opinion that 'It was a very good thing to mix the repertory. Strangely enough you didn't have two different audiences. You didn't have an audience which only liked dialect and an audience which only liked the non-dialect things. They took it all as exciting theatre.' But the dramatist, Jack Loudan, was there on the evening when, for a young American serviceman, the company's noted versatility didn't quite work: 'They were playing *The Drone* which is a short play and needs a curtain-raiser. On this occasion it was Chekhov's *The Proposal*. The curtain went down on the Chekhov and went up on *The Drone*. At the interval the young American came out and said to Joe Tomelty, "Look, I don't understand this. This thing starts off in Russia and lands in Co. Down." '

In the beginning, then, the various styles of acting did not fuse immediately or easily. Margaret D'Arcy recalls:

> There was a dialect group, a definite Northern Ireland group, and a group which you might call 'straight' actors. There was a feeling for a time that the dialect people didn't particularly like us and perhaps we were inclined to think that they were just playing themselves. But eventually we merged, very slowly for me, because it took a long time for anyone to accept me as someone who could speak with an Ulster accent.

As it turned out, this blending of talents and objectives was more than a compromise. Out of it came a style of acting intimately associated with the U.G.T. J. R. Mageean explains:

> When you have a group of actors working together for any length of time especially with the same producers, quite unconsciously a general style of acting forms itself. Of course, our actors were encouraged and helped to develop their individual styles as much as possible ... the result, intimate, natural, effortless acting.

This was particularly true of the work of R. H. McCandless, both as actor and producer. 'It was a deliberate style of acting that I adapted to myself and tried to get others to follow.' He succeeded by the most effective means of persuasion, his own artistry and hard work. Elizabeth Begley remembers coming off stage on the last night of a fifteen-week run of Patricia O'Connor's *The Farmer Wants a Wife*, and McCandless, the producer, '. . . called me over very confidentially and I thought "This is something nice he's going to say about my hard work." He said "Lily, you know that scene with the teacup? Well, play it out a little more with the cup before you speak." I didn't like to say "Bob, I don't play that scene again." That was Bob McCandless, he was never ever satisfied with a production.'

This fluency and flexibility of speech and movement grew out of, and in turn became the perfect complement to, the major part of the Group's work, the play set in Ulster. As Maurice O'Callaghan says of the dramatists who wrote for the Group: 'They wrote of themselves, of their people, of the soil; we were that. We couldn't be false to it, you can't be false to your own background. You must play it sincerely. Perhaps we weren't so sure of the foreign plays and our interpretation was slightly false. But we were sincere to the portrayal of our people.' To Alfred Arnold the acting in the plays of Shiels and Tomelty was a revelation: 'I used to watch them rehearsing and they didn't think consciously, I believe, that they were acting in a stylized way. They knew the background, the personalities, the life they were portraying. And they had the love of the language and the character which enabled them to project it just a little larger than life. It came over with the effect of complete naturalness. It was completely beguiling.'

There were, of course, failures as well as winners in the

history of the Group's productions. It's a commonplace that the play reader hasn't yet been born who can pick unerringly the winners in a pile of new plays. Broadly speaking, the Group Theatre was opposed to 'playing safe'. Over the years the willingness of the directors to offer their stage to a young playwright or a new play resulted in an impressive list of 'first performances'. (See Appendix II). This was particularly important to writers almost completely isolated from the theatre apart from the very occasional production in Dublin. As Patricia O'Connor, who contributed plays to the U.G.T. between 1942 and 1959, says:

> If it had not been for the Group Theatre I wouldn't have gone on. Sometimes one was discouraged, but the directors themselves were discouraged. Often the public didn't care for a play that appeared to us to be very good. We just had to accept that. I did find that, on the whole, they (the Directors) were interested and would discuss points with the author . . . R. H. McCandless had almost too high a regard for writers.

The war years brought many American and European lovers of the play to the small theatre in Bedford Street. James Bridie, stationed for a time in Belfast, admired the work of the U.G.T., gave them his three-act comedy *The Black Eye* to produce, and secured them seasons in 1946 and 1948 at the Glasgow Citizens' Theatre. In 1945 Tyrone Guthrie introduced the Ulster company to the Liverpool Playhouse where they returned in 1946. Between 1945 and 1957 the U.G.T. had seasons at the Gaiety Theatre, Dublin (1945), the Arts Theatre Club, London (1953), the Abbey Theatre, Dublin and the Opera House, Cork in 1954 and 1955, and the Repertory Theatre, Colchester in 1957. Sponsored by the Council for the Encouragement of Music and the Arts (later the Arts Council of Northern Ireland), they toured the Province on a number of occasions.

By 1950 significant changes had taken place in the activities and habits of the theatre-going public. 'We were in competition with broadcasting, T.V. and films,' says J. R. Mageean. 'Our actors were becoming well-known in Britain. We couldn't pay them enough to be able to ask them not to accept these offers.' In March 1951, after more than a decade of writing, acting and managing at the Group, Joseph Tomelty left for London with Tyrone Guthrie and the Northern Ireland Festival of Britain Company. His playing of John Fibbs in *The Passing Day* is now part of the story of Irish Theatre. He had been preceded by actors associated at one time or another with the U.G.T.; Alan McClelland, Bee Duffell, Lawrence Beattie. He was to be followed by many others, now distinguished names in theatre, radio and film; Patrick Magee, Harry Towb, J. G. Devlin, Patrick McAlliney, Denys Hawthorne, Stephen Boyd, Elizabeth Begley, Colin Blakely, Doreen Hepburn, James Ellis. It's a pipe dream, of course, to think of a play, a theatre and a producer that could muster this talented company for no matter how brief a time—but a pleasant one.

For some years the Group Theatre has been under the management of James Young and his partner, Jack Hudson. A comic actor of genius, Young, with every justification, has subtitled the Bedford Street theatre the 'Home of Ulster Comedy'. In plays such as Glen Melville's *The Love Market*, the Theatre has developed its own type of farcical comedy. John McDonnell has been the most prolific writer for the company with eight plays to date, each running to 200 performances or more. Young can inject a satirical tone into his work, not too corrosive perhaps, but he persuades his audiences to laugh at themselves, an altogether praiseworthy achievement. He would agree, I think, with Frank Reynolds the last manager of the old Empire who said he liked to see his audiences 'going out in better humour than when they came in—which is the true secret of entertainment.'

The Group and the U.L.T. were the two most influential companies in the first fifty years of the theatre in Ulster. If one remained adamantly amateur for over thirty years, the other strove, with some success, to make itself fully professional. The U.L.T. wrote most of their plays. The Group Theatre, as Joseph Tomelty has said, was, in many ways, a theatre workshop. Writers, most of them with little experience of the theatre, found actors and producers willing to give their work a chance. From 1940 to 1955 almost fifty plays made their first appearance on the stage of the Ulster Group Theatre.

5

Plays and Playwrights

From its beginnings in 1940 the Ulster Group Theatre was closely associated with the names of three dramatists, George Shiels, Joseph Tomelty and St John Ervine. 'There was no similarity between these writers,' says J. R. Mageean. 'We could produce a play by Shiels, follow it by an Ervine and after that a Tomelty. There you had three months, much more in some cases, of first-class entertainment. What a gift to any theatre!'

George Shiels, in his long creative life of thirty-two years in which time he wrote some twenty plays, contributed to three major Irish theatres. There was his 'prentice work for the U.L.T., the important middle period when as an 'Abbey dramatist' he gained his reputation in Europe and North America, and his association from 1940 with the U.G.T. Five plays were written in the Group period: *Macook's Corner* (1942), originally written for the Abbey Theatre as *Neal Maquade*, *The Old Broom* (1944), *Borderwine* (1946), *Mountain Post* (1948) and *Slave Drivers* (1950).

Apart from the plays themselves, evidence of Shiels's developing art as a dramatist can be found in the comments of critics and fellow-writers. In 1929, referring to the comedy *Professor Tim*, A. E. Malone wrote:

> There is no attempt to effect a contact with the life of Ireland in which the scene is supposed to be laid. The same is true of *Cartney and Kevney* which uses the well-worn stock characters in the time-honoured humorous situations. In all his plays the author tends to repeat himself, there is little plot or characterisation, and in none of the plays except *Paul Twyning* is there displayed more than a merely casual acquaintance with the realities of Irish peasant life. Perhaps in the future George Shiels may write a true comedy, but the disability which he suffers prevents that immersion in contemporary life from which true comedy must come.[1]

Ten years later T. C. Murray wrote of Shiels's ninth play, *The New Gossoon*:

> for all its comedy (it is) an interesting social document, for it mirrors the changing aspect of the Irish rural scene ... In Shiels's play we have the conflict of the two generations—the young, scornful of the traditional view of life and conduct; the old, shocked and bewildered as they observe the lack of regard for such cherished sanctities as submission to paternal control and the claim of the land to every atom of energy stored in healthy young bodies.[2]

Although confined to his home because of an accident suffered in his early years in Canada—the disability referred to by Malone—Shiels's perception and imagination were in no way circumscribed. When *The New Gossoon* was written the internal combustion engine had bellowed its way into a rural community that had changed little since the eighteenth century. Shiels heard it from his study window. Throughout the play Luke Cary's motorbike is always in the spectator's eye. 'This is a theme which has been under everyone's eyes for the past twenty years,' said Frank O'Connor, 'but Shiels was the man who pounced on it. He presented it with an authenticity which is rare in modern literature.'³

What at times troubled Shiels's admirers was not his lack of knowledge of Irish provincial life but the probing bitterness with which he delineated it. 'More like that of Swift,' said O'Connor, 'than of any other Irish writer.'

For example, in the scene between Ben Broom and Hubert in *The Old Broom* the playwright betrays no awareness of the obliquity of his characters—characters who seem to share precisely the same dubious moral values and yet who, dramatically, cannot be 'on the same side':

BEN: My daughter says you're a paragon of virtue, and my son Austin tells me you're the makings of a good lawyer. Which is one to believe?

HUBERT: (smiling) Perhaps a little of both.

BEN: Yes, but how much of each? If I knew where virtue ends and legal ability begins, I could easily forecast your future.

HUBERT: (chary) May not a virtuous man be a good lawyer?

BEN: He may, but he won't go very far in his profession. When I want legal advice I don't consult a paragon of virtue, I hire the slickest customer I can get.

HUBERT: I hesitate to say this, sir, and hope you won't misunderstand me. Is not a *show* of virtue a great business asset?

BEN: One of the greatest. But to carry it off one must have very exceptional gifts. Have you got those gifts?

HUBERT: I think they can be acquired.

BEN: Have you got a conscience?

HUBERT: Do you mean in business or in private life?

BEN: I mean both. The idea that you can put it off and on like an overcoat is a fallacy. I tried it myself.

HUBERT: All I shall say, sir, is this; I mean to get on in the world, and nothing is going to stand in my way.

BEN: Neither moral law nor any silly question of principle?

HUBERT: Neither.

BEN: Your most effective weapon is hypocrisy. Worm yourself into the confidence of friend and foe alike—into their very bowels. To do that you must be an ardent believer in hypocrisy.

HUBERT: As a matter of fact, sir, I am. But we call it finesse.

Seeing *Cartney and Kevney* on the Abbey stage, Yeats wrote: 'It displayed a series of base actions without anything to show that its author disapproved or expected us to do so. I left before the finish, feeling that neither I nor anyone else in that audience could help transferring to the author himself the horror inspired by his characters.' (I cannot resist placing beside this the remark of a Belfast's paper's London correspondent on the Northern Ireland Festival Company's production of *The Passing Day* at the Lyric Theatre, Hammersmith in 1951: 'As a Festival choice it may throw too much emphasis on the sinners, and, if taken too literally by the uninitiated, may even put doubly on his guard the business man who ventures across the Irish Sea.')[4]

We have seen more of Shiels than had Yeats back in 1927. For almost every one of his knaves we can counter with an admirable character. In *The Rugged Path* and *The Summit* there is the courage of Sean Tansey and the integrity of the police sergeant faced with the enmity of a brutalised mountainy family, themselves, as the playwright hints, victims of history. There is the compassion of the woman towards Dan Farran, the ex-convict in *The Jail-Bird*. There is the understanding and sympathy of the middle-aged farm hand, Ned Shay, for the new gossoon and his generation.

Lennox Robinson referred to Shiels as the Tom Moore of Irish drama. Other critics have decried him for his easy sentiment. But in those plays, probably the most important, where Shiels deals with the shoddier aspects of Irish life, there is little sentimentality. Irony is his weapon and he points it home with a smile—sometimes a savage one. 'The easy label "writer of comedy" does not fit Shiels,' wrote David Kennedy. He continued:

> True, it was in this role he packed the Abbey Theatre and village halls all over Ireland with laughter-loving audiences, but his own people in Ulster have seen a subtlety in his character-drawing and heard nuances in his dialogue which southern audiences missed. While he would have been the last man to deny that he was an Irishman, he was also an Ulsterman, and when he wrote for Ulstermen he used a finer brush and more delicate tints. For a wider public he kept closer to the primary colours.[5]

To many people Shiels still means the Group Theatre and those wonderful performances of R. H. McCandless, Elizabeth Begley and Joseph Tomelty. His plays, in David Kennedy's opinion, '... have nowhere been better interpreted than in Belfast. It is not a matter of acting and production only—these are often better done in Dublin—but of that invisible co-operation between audience and stage: nuances of expression and character arousing overtones of feeling, emotional harmonics, in the audience.'[6]

As far as the portrayal of love is concerned, St John Ervine is more accomplished than Shiels. In almost any play of Shiels's where the courtship of two of the principal characters is of more than marginal significance to the development of the drama one gets the impression that the affair was arranged by the village matchmaker, and that's that, so let's get to the entertaining skulduggery of the other characters. But in Ervine's *Friends and Relations* there is a perceptible development in the relationship between Jenny Conn and Adam Bothwell. *Martha*, which he gave to the Group Theatre in 1955, portrays a somewhat similar relationship brought this time into the foreground as the major theme but played against the selfishness, greed and weakness of Martha's middle-class family. Margaret D'Arcy, I recall, was outstanding in the part of Martha, a daughter devoted to the care of a family who take her too much for granted.

It has been said that in *Martha* and particularly in *Friends and Relations* Ervine set out to satirise the Belfast middle-class. When the latter play was revived at the U.G.T. in 1951, one critic, having remarked that the Ulster theatre was not accustomed to plays that criticised this section of the community, continued: 'A certain amount of philosophisation is necessarily the basis of *Friends and Relations* because the play sets out to present several contrasting mentalities and outlooks, with faults and good points side by side, in such a way as to make the play deep as well as entertaining . . . it is a good play in spite of its depth sometimes intruding on the plot.'[7] If the play's depth eludes us today so does its satire. Indeed in the famous posthumous letter Sir Samuel Lepper upbraids his 'friends and relations' for having neglected the admirable bourgeois qualities of industry, sobriety and keeping an eye on the pennies growing into pounds.

> Well, that's all I have to say about you, friends and relations. I can't say it would have been any loss if I'd never seen one of you. I'd be a lot better off if I hadn't . . . I was only fit to

be rich and surrounded by sycophants and spongers. That's
the punishment every rich man receives. It's his hell on earth
and you've all been mine. I feel I've done you enough harm
by maintaining you when I'd have done better to let you
earn your own living, and I can't go comfortably to my
grave with the thought in my head that I'm completing your
ruin by leaving you all I have.[8]

Several of Ervine's 'English' plays such as *Robert's Wife*
were performed by the U.G.T. But it was his Ulster plays that
drew the audiences: *My Brother Tom* (1952), *Ballyfarland's
Festival* (1953), a dramatisation by John Boyd of Ervine's
novel *Mrs Martin's Man* (1954), *Martha* (1955) and the
earlier plays, *Friends and Relations* and *John Ferguson* memorable in the Group production for R. H. McCandless's fine
speaking of David's lament over Absalom. (The Ulster Protestant may be chary of rhetoric but when it's unavoidable there's
always an apt passage in the Bible.) But first in popular favour
was *Boyd's Shop*. 'It brings to the stage,' writes David Kennedy,
'the Presbyterian middle class which in the past has received
more kicks than ha'pence from the Irish dramatists. It is seen
through the rose-tinted spectacles of the exile. Presbyterian
Ulster liked this picture of itself . . . sentimental, yes, but a
little sentiment was needed here to neutralise a former excess of
acid.'[9]

T. G. F. Patterson, the Irish antiquarian, records that in one
of George Russell's notebooks there is 'a tale about the ghosts
of the dead walking on All Hallows' Eve . . . From the manu-
script it is clear that he intended forming the notes into a play,
but I do not think he ever did so.'[10] Joseph Tomelty heard the
same tale in his childhood, not among the orchard slopes of
Armagh but by the fanged seacoast of Down, and wrote his
play *All Souls' Night*. The swept hearth and plenished fire of

the tradition, therefore, are those of a family of fisherfolk, the Quinns. But the spirits who walk at the end of the play are not ancestral but ghosts new-minted, for through her avarice Katrine the mother drives her two sons to their death in the waters of the lough. Tomelty, born in the fishing village of Portaferry, nets love and death and greed and fish and birds and boats in a heightened language that comes as naturally from his characters as the flow of tides in Strangford Lough. *All Souls' Night* is a tragedy but probably the most memorable scene is that in which John Quinn, the father, illiterate, learns to cipher: 'so that's a nought, round like a sail ring or the eye of a herring. And that's a five, shaped like a cup hook in the dresser, and a six like what a worm would ooze on the beach . . . ' Those who saw the author play the old fisherman, his voice hushed in awe and delight at his discovery, will not easily forget the scene.

A number of Tomelty's plays are unobtainable, but he has written, as far as I can discover, thirteen: *Barnum was Right* (1939), *Idolatry at Inishargie* (1942), *Poor Errand* (1943), *Right Again, Barnum* (1943), *The End House* (1944), *All Souls' Night* (1949), *Down the Heather Glen* (1952), *Mugs and Money* (1953), *Is the Priest at Home?* (1954), *April in Assagh* (1954), *To Have a Little House* (1956), *Year at Marlfield* (1965) and *Spring in September* (1966). *Barnum was Right* was first produced by the N.I.P. at the Empire Theatre as already noted, the fifth in the list at the Abbey Theatre, Dublin, the seventh at the Arts Theatre, Belfast, the ninth at the Opera House, Belfast, the tenth at the New Theatre, Bangor, the eleventh at the Grove Theatre, Belfast, the thirteenth at the Circle Theatre, Belfast, and the others at the Group Theatre.

According to a contributor to the *Pelican Guide to English Literature*, 'many playwrights have dealt in the Ibsen manner with the typical problems of modern Irish life'.[11] He lists these problems, assigning to Tomelty (with Paul Vincent Carroll) that of 'the role of the priests'. I should add that Joseph Tomelty does not agree that any of his work falls into this category. He has written two plays on the daily trials and triumphs of Father Malan, priest-in-charge of his flock in the village of Marlfield. The second of these—*Year at Marlfield*—was only moderately successful when it was presented by a group sponsored by the Arts Council of Northern Ireland, the Ulster Theatre Company. The earlier play *Is the Priest at Home?* has become one of Tomelty's most popular plays.

The End House, the last house in a Belfast street, is inhabited by the MacAstockers, a family caught up in the travail of murderous political strife. The gable wall is pockmarked with bullet holes where an informer has been shot down. Seamus the son has recently been released from jail and is to die violently. The elder generation cling to the small civilities of life amid threats, raids and poverty. In 1944 Tomelty told a reporter that he had begun the play as far back as 1932. It was set aside for some years while he wrote for the Group Theatre. Then he decided that the earlier play must be finished because 'it was time people outside got an idea of how things were in Belfast'.[12] *The End House* opened at the Abbey Theatre in August, 1944. It has not yet, I believe, had a professional production in Belfast.

The Dublin critics of *The End House*, while agreeing on the quality of the play, were not of a mind as to the author's 'mood'. Gabriel Fallon in the *Standard* felt that Tomelty had plumbed too deeply in despair. 'He has decided for naturalism, and forced the poverty and pride and patriotism and per-secution of one Belfast household into a dialogue which though it suited his purpose well enough and carried a thin humour at

7

times, lacked even a tittle of ... poetic luxuriance ... '[13] The
Irish Times, on the other hand, decided that 'the play is very
strongly in the O'Casey tenement tradition and Mr Tomelty
plays strongly on the oppression and persecution theme. He
leavens the tragedy and sordidness with a rich vein of
humour.'[14]

I do not think that anyone today would hesitate to associate
himself with the second of these comments. There was a time
indeed when it seemed that audiences were to enjoy the sheer
inventiveness of this writer's dialogue at the expense of the
play. One critic observed about his fourth play, *Right Again,
Barnum*, that 'what is new here is the shapeliness of the drama,
the checking of the sprightly wry humour that in previous
efforts has carried the author away from his theme and caused
dissatisfaction as though he had not troubled himself sufficiently with his plot'. Tomelty is unrivalled among his contemporaries in the use of the idiomatic phrase. At a time when we
were surfeited perhaps with the prosaic exchanges of the
characters of Ervine and Shiels he brought lyricism to the
speech of the Ulster stage.

One of Hugh Quinn's full-length plays, *Legacy of Delight*
(1943), had its first run at the Group Theatre. The legacy of the
title comes unexpectedly to a working-class family, the
McFalls, and the play chronicles the upsets that it brings to
their lives, in their ascent from Sardinia Street, Shankill Road,
to Derrygowan Manor and back to the Shankill Road. Quinn
is best remembered as the author of *Mrs McConaghy`s Money*,
first produced at the Abbey Theatre under its original title
Money on 9 March 1931. With Rutherford Mayne's *Bridgehead*
and the Shiels duo *The Rugged Path* and *The Summit* it is, in my
opinion, one of the three best plays written by Ulster dramatists

in the first half of the century. Introducing a collection of Quinn's plays, St John Ervine remarks on

> their fidelity to Belfast working-class life. But they are more than faithful to the mere facts of that life: they illuminate it. Hugh Quinn extraordinarily reveals the thoughts of his characters, and is not content, as some authors are, merely to show their actions ... Quinn catches the character of his people with singular swiftness. He does not waste any time in building up 'characters'; he allows his people to display their nature without any assistance from the theatre.[15]

St John Ervine comments on the fact that none of Hugh Quinn's plays was produced by the Ulster Players (the U.L.T.). Jack Loudan whose first full-length play, *The Ball Turns Once*, was produced at the Grand Opera House, Belfast and at the Abbey Theatre, Dublin in 1935 brings back to our story a name well-known to the Ulster Players, that of Whitford Kane. Kane produced Loudan's play in New York. 'The story behind the production', the playwright says, 'was that he'd heard of the Ulster Players' production, got a script from me and decided on a New York production. The play got good notices but did not move into Broadway. It remained at the Lennox Theatre, a kind of try-out rather like the Lyric Theatre in Hammersmith.'

Loudan contributed four plays to the U.G.T.: *Story for Today* (1941), *Henry Joy McCracken* (1945), *A Lock of the General's Hair* (1953) and in the same year *In Donegall Square*, an adaptation of Philip and Aimee Stuart's *Nine Till Six*. In 1958, following the controversy between some members of the U.G.T. management and the playwright Sam Thompson, Loudan, in protest, withdrew a new play *Trouble in the Square* from the Theatre. In 1951, at the invitation of Tyrone Guthrie, he adapted Shadwell's *The Sham Prince* for the Northern Ireland Festival Company's season in London.

Henry Joy McCracken, a costume play of 1798, like Carn-duff's *Castlereagh*, tells of the trial and execution of the young Belfast merchant who led the United Irishmen at the battle of Antrim. In *Story for Today*, like Tomelty's *Poor Errand*, the devastating air raids on Belfast are an agent in complicating or resolving the problems in the lives of the characters. In Loudan's third play, a light-hearted affair set in today's Ulster, the 'lock of hair' is a relic of another leader in the 1798 Rising, General Harry Munro. This play, notable for its ingenious stagecraft, is a comedy, but through it runs a plea for a more enlightened Ireland. As Bill Morton, the narrator-journalist, says to Miss Dolly Munro, the last and charming keeper of the heirloom:

> We're not like other nations. The French or the Americans can have their fourteenth of July or their Independence Day, because they embody ideals which every Frenchman or American accepts. But in Ireland there's nothing in the past that we can celebrate together. There are only years of bitter-ness and misunderstanding . . . I suppose we're still reaping the harvest of the past. What good will it do us to remember King James or King William, the Siege of Limerick or Robert Emmet, if it closes our eyes to the things we should be doing for our country today?[16]

The U.G.T. presented Patricia O'Connor's first play *Highly Efficient* in 1942. It caused some stir and understandably so for it was a courageous and pungent assault on the antediluvian method of teaching in elementary schools. 'This play was written by a teacher,' says the author in the foreword to the published play, 'about teachers for teachers . . . it was the interest of the general public, however, that seemed the most significant feature in the experiment both to me and to the other teachers with whom I discussed it. Another encouraging feature was that a commercial theatre was found in Belfast prepared to produce a play concerned solely with the subject of Public Elementary Education.'[17]

Highly Efficient could be called a wry comedy. Apart from the idealistic young teacher, Margaret Henderson, we meet few attractive characters in the village of Ballydim. There's the Rev. Mr McFee, as doltish a school manager as ever stepped in clerical boots, William Davidson who doesn't find illiteracy an insurmountable obstacle to his activities on the school committee, and Miss Burke, a fellow-teacher, disillusioned and cynical, who tells Margaret that 'you can take it from me the William Davidsons were produced by a so-called education system that was deliberately *planned* for the purpose of producing William Davidsons ... the people who planned it are long ago discredited; they don't matter, but their plans are still intact, and William Davidson and Co. will see that they are carried out'. The 'plans' aren't so intact today and I have no doubt that *Highly Efficient* and its author can take some of the credit for that. Patricia O'Connor wrote a number of other plays for the Group Theatre: *Voice out of Rama* (1943), which deals with the drift to the towns, *Select Vestry* (1945), the impact of big business on church affairs, *Master Adams* (1949), *The Farmer Wants a Wife* (1955), *Who Saw Her Die?* (1957) and *The Sparrows Fall* (1959).

Between 1940 and 1960 a number of writers whose output of plays may not have been so numerous or sustained as those already mentioned in this chapter contributed notably to Ulster drama. There is room here to mention only a few. Harry S. Gibson, whose activity in the theatre as playwright and actor extends over many years, contributed two successful

plays to the U.G.T.: *Bannister's Café* (1949) and *The Square
Peg* (1950). Another active writer was Cecil Cree whose first
play *The House that Jack Built* was produced at the Group in
1948. His *Title for Buxey* (1949) in which he took the fight
game as his theme gave the U.G.T. one of its most memorable
and long-running plays. Michael J. Murphy, the short story
writer and folklorist, brought from his native South Armagh a
fresh lilt to the speech of the stage. In 1953 his tragedy *Dust
Under Our Feet* was taken by the Group to the Arts Theatre,
London, at the request of Alec Clunes, the Theatre's adminis-
trator. His *Men on the Wall* (1960) was produced at the Group
and the Abbey Theatres, and a one-acter, *The Hard Man*, at
the Abbey Experimental Theatre. P. S. Loughlin contributed
to *Harrap's One-Act Plays 1950–1*, and his three-act play
Waiting Night was given its première at the Abbey Theatre in
1957. When the Northern Ireland Festival Company opened
for a season at the Lyric Theatre, Hammersmith in 1951
Tyrone Guthrie took with him a new play *Danger, Men
Working*, the first stage venture of a young Ulster writer, John
D. Stewart. In 1953 this play, revised, was toured by the
U.G.T. Stewart lived abroad for some years but continued to
write for television and radio. His latest work in this field is the
television comedy *Boatman Do Not Tarry* which he has
adapted for the stage. He was co-author of the satirical revue
A State of Chassis presented last year at the Peacock Theatre,
Dublin. These three writers have contributed outstanding
work to the drama and features departments of the BBC.

In August 1958 the curtain of the Belfast Opera House rose
on a play which was to leave its mark on the future of the
drama in Ulster long after its merits or faults as a piece of
theatre writing were forgotten. The occasion was the U.G.T.
presentation of a tragedy about the 'hatred between Catholics

and Protestants in Ulster,' written by Gerard McLarnon, a Yorkshireman of Irish parentage. It was called *The Bonefire* and if the letters written to the Press by a handful of its first-night audience were to be trusted, it threatened to spread into a conflagration. It didn't do anything of the sort, of course. (Gerald Macnamara, with his satirical comedies, had discovered this half-a-century earlier.) The audiences gave their close attention to the play and their unstinted applause to Tyrone Guthrie's brilliant production and the acting of Maurice O'Callaghan, Catherine Gibson, Margaret D'Arcy, James Ellis, J. G. Devlin and Colin Blakely.

A critic wrote of the play: 'Though it is a striking—at times superlative—piece of theatre, it does not rise above the problem it states. Little solace emerges from its anguish; small dignity survives its orgiastic flames. It is a vomit of disgust . . . a foreigner seeing this presentation by the Group Theatre company at the Edinburgh Festival next month will not react to it as would an Ulster Catholic or an Ulster Protestant. He will not regard the Orange bigots and the spineless Catholics on the stage as crude caricatures. The challenge of the author will seem to him to be directed to all humanity, not just our riven community. But we, who see the play in Belfast, are prisoners within the skins we wore when we were baptised. The fault of this play, on the purely local plane, is that it does nothing to release us. It offers too little hope, and of despair we have too much already.'[18]

Into this atmosphere of aroused public awareness of the theatre erupted a playwright given much more to hope than to despair. Sam Thompson had written a number of radio scripts dealing with life in the shipyards and in the working-class districts of Belfast. In 1957 he completed his first stage play and offered it to the U.G.T., whose management had changed considerably since its early days. The play was accepted. The author was then asked to delete or alter some passages in his script. This he refused to do and the play was withdrawn from production by the Theatre management. So far as the story of the controversial play on the Ulster stage was concerned, the Group board had evidently learnt nothing and forgotten a lot. Defending their decision they stated that they were 'determined not to mount any play which would offend or affront the religious or political beliefs or sensibilities of the man in the street of any denomination or class in the community and which would give rise to sectarian or political controversy of an extreme nature'.

This pronouncement, a 'staggering repudiation of drama as a serious art form', as Stewart Parker puts it,[19] hastened the disintegration of the U.G.T. A number of the Theatre directors resigned, Jack Loudan withdrew a play in protest, public interest was aroused, Thompson had an action for breach of contract settled in his favour out of court—and was left without a theatre for his play. Once upon a time Bernard Shaw wrote to tell Hugh Quinn that if he had the wit to write a play he had the wit to get it on. Sam Thompson proceeded, energetically, to prove the wisdom of this conclusion and his play, produced by James Ellis, opened at the Empire Theatre, Belfast, on 26 January 1960.

The objections to *Over the Bridge* were partly due to its idiomatic dialogue, and even more to its author's uncompromising determination to state in dramatic terms the full horror of bigotry, mob violence, death. The objectors asserted that fear of these things had receded long ago. Thompson maintained that it hadn't. The action of the play is centred on the dilemma of a group of trade union officials faced with an outbreak of sectarianism among their fellow-workers. The author knew his trade unionists; he had been a shop steward. He knew the shipyard and the men who worked there and drew on it as other writers draw on the life of a town:

MARIAN: Father's always telling me that the pattern of all Belfast life is to be found in the shipyard. Does Rabbie believe that, Martha?

MARTHA: Every word of it. Rabbie tells me that down there you get the two extremes. From the devout Christians to the fellows who would steal the Lord's supper.

Davey Mitchell, reserved, honest, totally fearless, has given his days to the cause of his craft union. He is to give his life. Faced by a murderous mob he walks out side by side with Peter O'Boyle to the work bench. Before he goes out to his death he turns to his comrades:

DAVEY: All my life I've fought for the principles of my union and Peter, here, fought for them, too. Would you want me to refuse to work with him because he upholds what is his right, to work without intimidation?

RABBIE: We all uphold that, Davey, but this is a mob we're dealing with. Mobs don't reason.

DAVEY: If I refuse to go out there and stand alongside my mate at that bench, everything I've ever fought for or believed in has been nothing.

For six weeks *Over the Bridge* drew packed and enthusiastic audiences to the Empire Theatre, then it went on tour to Dublin, Scotland and England. Amid the opinions engendered by the play it was possible to detect a quite extraordinary feeling of relief that at last the unclean spirit of sectarianism had been dragged before the footlights and examined with passion, pity and corrosive laughter. Thompson discovered, as had Ibsen, that 'no dramatist lives through anything in isolation. What he lives through all his countrymen live through with him'.

His second play, *The Evangelist*, was presented at the Belfast Opera House on 3 June 1963. The playwright's original intention was to examine another facet of the problem stated in the earlier play, the central figure this time being a politico-cleric noted more for agitation than *agape*. But as the play grew under his hand it became evident that he was creating a different, but equally valid figure, the peripatetic evangelist with a streamlined Madison Avenue technique. That first production is memorable for many reasons but chiefly for the tremendous detonation of the gospel hall scene in the first act and the consummate acting of Ray McAnally as Pastor Earls, the evangelist. Reviewing the play, Ralph Bossence said: 'Never has the technique of the modern religious spell-binder been more faithfully observed. The gospel hall scene is a magnificent piece of theatre in the writing, the production by Hilton Edwards and the dominating performance of Mr McAnally, who presents God as the great managing director and the Bible as the union card securing admission to heaven, thus straddling both sides of the industrial fence . . . make this the most exciting sequence in the play. It is run a close second by the curtain scene of the first act in which Mr Thompson, playing the agnostic part of Manser Brown, defies Pastor Earls from a first floor window. The dialogue here is meant to shock and succeeds, but it is a legitimate dramatic device to oppose the smooth syrup of the evangelist with the earthy mockery of his opponent. The author deserves full praise for his courage in tackling such a theme. He does not disguise where his sympathies lie—with ordinary decency and love and understanding against false and commercialised religion—and it was clear from the reception which his play received that he struck a responsive chord in his audience.'[20]

His third major play, *Cemented with Love*, was written for television. The irony of the title is sustained as the playwright dissects with glee the corruption, nepotism and general skulduggery practised by the traditional parties during an election in the constituency of Drumtory. The play was accepted by the BBC but the author was again to suffer the frustration of delay and postponement. *Cemented with Love* was eventually screened in April 1965, two months after the death of its author. A stage version of the play was presented at the 1967 Dublin Theatre Festival.

After Sam Thompson's untimely death in 1965 a fourth play, almost completed, was discovered. Titled *The Masquerade*, it reveals an impressive effort by the playwright to free himself, temporarily at least, from the trammels of the Ulster scene. 'The play opens in a basement house in London,' runs the stage direction. 'Half of the basement to the right is decorated with Nazi emblems . . . a huge swastika hangs from the ceiling.' Other furnishings include 'an oak coffin open to the audience, a shoeshine block with a pair of highly-polished jackboots and a pair of lady's black high-heeled shoes'. *The Masquerade* is played out by three main characters, Suzanne, a call girl, 'Obergruppenfuehrer' Frank Major, a psychopathic thug, and Herbert Manly, Major's amanuensis, for ever inditing for his master long letters to Goering, Himmler and Heydrich, 'dead, dead for nearly twenty years'. The script, even in this draft, reveals that most exciting phenomenon, an adventurous and creative mind setting out on a journey of exploration.

There is no evidence, to the present, that any dramatist is

following in Thompson's footsteps. They may lack his indignation, his creative stamina and his knowledge. There are signs that the horizon which he cleared for his fellow-writers is being exploited by a number of radical young Ulster poets. In a tribute to the playwright, broadcast shortly after his death, a speaker said: 'Looking back now, one can see more clearly why the play (*Over the Bridge*) made the impact that it did. George Shiels, St John Ervine and many lesser lights had dominated the Ulster theatre for over thirty years. They were skilful technicians whose dramas were enacted in the kitchen and the drawing-room by people whose ideas were old-fashioned and a little remote from reality by today's standards. *Over the Bridge* knocked down the kitchen wall and brought the streets and the shipyard on to the stage. The domestic wrangles between youth and age, greed and idealism, which had been the themes of the earlier dramatists, were replaced by the bitter arguments and antagonisms of men rotted by bigotry and hardship. All the uglier aspects of our communal life were brought to the surface and the Ulster theatre could never be quite the same again.'[21]

By the fifties our younger dramatists discarded, some abruptly, the perspectives and problems that had been exploited so successfully in the theatre of the previous two decades. The post-war world that they set themselves to observe had altered unrecognisably from that peopled by Andrew Boyd, Ben Broom and Mrs McConaghy. Radio, television and the pioneer efforts of theatre-workers like Hubert Wilmot and Mary O'Malley brought them news of a different and exciting theatre. From Lewis Purcell to Joseph Tomelty—a period of fifty years—it is possible without too much effort to trace a continuous idiom of speech and theme. The writers of today discover in themselves no allegiance to this 'tradition'. Even the

cherished accolade of the Ulster playwright, 'an Abbey production', has lost some of its lustre. David McGibbon, a young
writer whose *Milligan* was produced at the Circle Theatre,
Belfast, in 1965, was awarded a grant from the Arts Council of
Northern Ireland to work for a year at the Royal Court
Theatre in London. Before he left he wrote to me to say: 'In
Northern Ireland I can find no minds to follow, no tradition of
theatre to build on. I find myself working in a void.' Not
all his contemporaries would agree with McGibbon: but it is
evident that dramatic writing in Ulster is moving towards,
and is prepared to take its chance in, a wider world of the
theatre.

When Stewart Love's *Randy Dandy* was presented at the
Group Theatre in January 1960, a critic wrote: 'in Stewart
Love we have a talented young playwright who can bring to
Ulster drama the realism, the authenticity and the fresh outlook
of which it is in such need'. The critics couldn't agree on the
play itself. 'Good idea goes to waste', announced one. 'Promising start for new author', decided another. '*The Randy Dandy*
looks back in ponderous anger', declared a third. (Almost all
the critics agreed that comparison with John Osborne's Jimmy
Porter was inevitable.) They also agreed on the importance of
the play.

'Dandy' Jordan, a shipyard worker who prefers poetry to
porter, has a hunger beyond anything that his home can offer,
including fish and chips in a newspaper. He views his wife with
a pitying affection, his mother-in-law with disgust, and makes a
fresh evaluation every morning of the men with whom he
works. His is the only voice raised against an unofficial strike.
It could have earned him a beating-up. But 'if you've anything
to say you should always say it. You should stand up every so
often and blare out your opinions. Let them hear you. Let

them know you're awake. Let them know that they're not going to walk and trample all over you'.

Stewart Love is as familiar with working-class life as were Tom Carnduff, Hugh Quinn or Sam Thompson. The two earlier playwrights, for all the honesty and poignancy of their characterisation, were inhibited by political quietism. Plays like Carnduff's *Traitors* stirred their audiences to cry 'Ah, the pity of it!' before dispersing to their comfortable homes. The last thing Sam Thompson asked for was pity, nor even 'justice'. He wanted *change*. In his plays we look through the eyes of Davey Mitchell and Manser Brown, men who wear their incorruptibility not like a hair shirt but like their own skin. Stewart Love portrays their enemies, within their own class, men maimed by a society that has made them Jack-all-alone. Randy Jordan's outburst against the wildcat strikers is a general denunciation of a drear existence peopled by only-too-fallible fellow-beings: 'I think it's a bad thing when you begin to take things for granted. Just to go to work and come home again and live and breathe and argue and fight and then just die without leaving a trace, just like you'd never existed ... you never even ripple the water. I want more than that.'

Joe, in *The Big Donkey*, sacked and mortally afraid of being thrown on the scrap heap, betrays his mate and his fellow-workers. When his wife pleads with him not to press a debt owed by Eddie his best friend, also unemployed and with a pregnant wife, Joe answers:

JOE: Look, I'm not the brightest fella that ever walked down Royal Avenue. If I was as bright as I would like to be I wouldn't have been a burner in the shipyard in the first place. But I can count. I know what's mine and what's somebody else's. This is mine, that's yours, and you're not getting any of mine.

ISOBEL: I've never heard you talk like this before.

JOE: What are you talking about? That's the way I live every day of the week . . .

And in his pursuit of a job he is quite willing to undersell his mates:

JOE: You employ burners here?

MORGAN: No, son, we do it with tin openers.

JOE: How much do you pay them?
   (Morgan looks up without a word. Joe pauses and comes to a decision. Slowly he swallows his pride and betrays himself.)
   Mister, I'll work for less.

MORGAN: Go on home, son. I don't want to know you.

Then when he has repulsed his father and stolen his friend's job he stands before his wife speaking 'as a man who knows exactly what he has done':

JOE: Isobel, I took Eddie's job. I took Eddie's money. I know this. But I acted as a responsible man. I have destroyed a whole small world of people, things which will never grow again. I know this. Things are dead which once I knew. Don't join them, please, Isobel.

The Big Donkey was first presented as a stage play by the Ulster Theatre Company at the Troxy (later the Grove) Theatre, Belfast, on 2 November 1964. A third stage play *The Big Long Bender*, described by a critic as '. . . portraying a group of young flat-dwellers, bent on having a good time without the unease and responsibility of any real relationship', was taken by the Queen's Players (of Queen's University,

Belfast) to the 1962 Edinburgh Festival and was given its Irish première at the Abbey Experimental Theatre, Dublin on 7 November 1964. A number of Stewart Love's plays have been televised. *The Big Donkey* was originally written for television and *The Randy Dandy* was picked by *The Listener* as one of the five best plays of 1961.

In the mid-sixties young writers could hope to see their work on the stage of the Circle Theatre, Belfast. *Snow Wedding* (1966) by Isobel Donaldson, and in 1965 David McGibbon's *Milligan* and John Hamilton's *He That Plays the King* were produced at this little playhouse. The Queen's University Dramatic Society staged McGibbon's *A Time of Change* at the 1968 Belfast Festival. This writer, now living in England, has turned his attention with some success to television drama. In 1963 Hamilton's *The Jesus Revolution* incurred the Lord Chamberlain's disapproval when taken by the Queen's company to the Edinburgh Festival. The same company's offering for the 1965 Belfast Festival was *A Song of the Albatross* by Hamilton, described by one critic as 'the outstanding event in the Festival's drama calendar.' Only on radio has John Hamilton's work been given professional production. The return of Hamilton and Stewart Love to writing for the stage would be greatly to the advantage of the theatre in Ulster.

Patrick Riddell's *House of Mallon* was produced at the U.G.T. in 1952. As a play about the Big House, in the Lennox Robinson manner, it was only partly successful, but it was an interesting attempt to break away from the rural drama so thoroughly worked by Shiels and his imitators. In 1968 Delta Productions staged his *Defence in Depth* at the Grove Theatre, Belfast, with Andre van Gyseghem in the lead. This play which had a television production by Radio Telefis Eireann was originally written for radio, a medium to which Riddell has contributed many scripts—the latest of them a comedy, *Mr Labby's Last Case*.

Another writer whose name appears in the U.G.T. list of plays is John Boyd; his adaptation of St John Ervine's novel *Mrs Martin Man* was produced by the Group in 1954. As their contribution to the 1967 Belfast Festival the Circle Theatre staged his play *The Blood of Colonel Lamb*. In 1969, this play, rewritten as *The Assassin*, was performed with notable success at the Dublin Theatre Festival. A reading of his new work *The Flats* in the Lyric Theatre's Sunday evening series was so well received by the audience that it was scheduled for production. The play which opened on 15 March 1971 is sub-titled 'Belfast 1971'. The action takes place in the Donellan household in a flats tower and covers a day of the comings and goings of the family in a district 'enduring bloodshed, anarchy and violence'. Through the younger members of the Donellan family and their friends the author succeeds in giving voice to the idealism, courage and bewilderment of a generation entering into a bitter heritage of hatred and greed. In the cast, Kathleen McClay as the young Protestant neighbour who dies to a sniper's bullet, and Pat Brannigan as Gerard Donellan, the idealistic student son, were outstanding.

John Boyd has stressed that *The Flats* is not a 'documentary'. Not being averse to the imaginative treatment of factual material, I think that he does himself an injustice. But in conversation with him it seems that he holds to a personal definition of the word. Certainly his audiences went away better informed on their fellow-citizens harrowed under by bloodshed, anarchy and violence—so much so that to meet public demand the Lyric Players revived the play later in the season.

The number of new plays seen at Belfast theatres in recent years has been depressingly small. One was Wesley Burrowes'

8

The Becauseway, a play in the Absurdist genre which was presented at the Lyric Theatre and which won an Irish Life Drama Award. Burrowes' *A Loud Bang on June 1st* (also an Irish Life Award winner) was scheduled for production at the Abbey Theatre in February 1971.

An article written some time ago on the future of the Gaiety Theatre, Dublin, referred to the popularity of the plays of John B. Keane, and continued: 'the only other playwrights at present capable of filling a theatre of the size of the Gaiety for any period are probably O'Casey, Brian Friel (since he became a Broadway success) and Hugh Leonard'. Brian Friel won his success in New York with his play in three episodes, *Philadelphia, Here I Come!* which was first performed on 28 September 1964 under Hilton Edwards' direction at the Gaiety Theatre during the Dublin Theatre Festival. Irish, American and English critics immediately acknowledged the arrival of a major dramatist, and the reception given to *Philadelphia* in New York confirmed this. Earlier plays were *This Doubtful Paradise* written in 1959 and staged at the U.G.T., *The Enemy Within*, produced at the Abbey Theatre in September 1962, and *The Blind Mice*, at the Eblana Theatre, Dublin, in February 1963— a play which has now been withdrawn by its author.

The Enemy Within is set on the Iona of Columba. One interpretation of this play, it seems to me, is that the 'enemy' is the thorn of princely pride forever pricking the flesh of the man of God. In the folk-tales about the nobly-born cleric there is a quality in his behaviour, arrogant and yet endearing, that is lacking in that of his fellow-saint, Patrick. But we know something of the insatiable political demands—including a call to bloodshed—made upon him by his family, even after his exile. It is no light task to breathe life into a stained-glass window; those who saw the production at the Lyric Theatre, or Tom Fleming's fine portrayal of Columba in the television version of the play, will not soon forget the warrior-saint's agonising renunciation of his kin and their feuds for the lonelier conflict of the missionary's cell and calling.

Philadelphia, Here I Come! is acknowledged as the finest play to have been written by an Ulster dramatist for many years—I am tempted to add since those of the playwright's fellow-Derryman, George Farquhar! Reviewing the published play[22] Sir Tyrone Guthrie said of its author: 'When one says that Brian Friel is a born playwright, what does it mean? It means that meaning is implicit "between the lines" of the text; in silences; in what people are thinking and doing far more than in what they are saying; in the music as much as in the meaning of a phrase. If you want to know what makes a born playwright, read the scene between Gareth and his old schoolmaster.'[23]

In the scene referred to, Master Boyle, 'around sixty, white-haired, handsome, defiant . . . shabbily dressed,' comes to bid goodbye to his former pupil Gareth O'Donnell, leaving for America next morning. There is affection between the two, Boyle indeed might have married pretty Maire Gallagher and been Gareth's father. The public Gareth that we see is shadowed by his other, private, self—sardonic, watchful, admonitory, unseen and unheard by the other characters. On the stage the two characters hold up the mirror to each other and to the small world of Ballybeg. As a device, says Guthrie, it 'works brilliantly for comedy and enables the author to get across a great deal of information and comment in a fascinating and economical way. It is a modification, you might say an elaboration, of the soliloquy.'

BOYLE: You're doing the right thing, of course. You'll never regret it. I gather it's a vast restless place that doesn't give a curse about the past; and that's the way things should be. Impermanence and anonymity—it offers great attractions . . . I didn't tell you, did I, that I may be going out there myself?

PRIVATE: Poor bastard.

BOYLE: I've been offered a big post in Boston, head of education in a reputable university there. They've given me three months to think it over. What are you going to do?

PUBLIC: Work in an hotel.

BOYLE: You have a job waiting for you?

PUBLIC: In Philadelphia.

BOYLE: . . . you're going to stay with friends?

PUBLIC: With Aunt Lizzy.

BOYLE: Of course.

PRIVATE: Go on. Try him.

PUBLIC: You knew her, didn't you, Master?

BOYLE: Yes, I knew all the Gallagher girls: Lizzy, Una, Rose, Agnes . . .

PRIVATE: And Maire, my mother, did you love her?

BOYLE: A long, long time ago . . . in the past . . . Do you remember the Christmas you sent me the packet of cigarettes? And the day you brought me a pot of jam to the digs? It was you, wasn't it?

PRIVATE: Poor Boyle—

BOYLE: All children are born with generosity. Three months they gave me to make up my mind.

PUBLIC: I remember very well—

BOYLE: By the way (*producing a small book*)—a little something to remind you of your old teacher—my poems—

PUBLIC: Thank you very much.

BOYLE: I had them printed privately last month. Some of them are a bit mawkish but you'll not notice any distinction.

PUBLIC: I'm very grateful, Master.

BOYLE: I'm not going to give you advice, Gar . . . But I would suggest that you strike out on your own as soon as you find your feet out there. Don't keep looking back over your shoulder. Be a hundred per cent American.

PUBLIC: I'll do that.

BOYLE: There's an inscription on the fly-leaf. By the way, Gar, you couldn't lend me ten shillings until—ha—I was going to say until next week but you'll be gone by then.

PUBLIC: Surely, surely.

PRIVATE: Give him the quid.

(*Public gives over a note. Boyle does not look at it*).

BOYLE: Fine. I'll move on now. Yes, I knew all the Gallagher girls from Bailtefree, long, long ago. Maire and Una and Rose and Lizzy and Agnes and Maire, your mother . . .

PRIVATE: You might have been my father.

BOYLE: . . . good luck, Gareth.

PUBLIC: Thanks, Master.

BOYLE: Forget Ballybeg and Ireland.

PUBLIC: It's easier said.

BOYLE: Perhaps you'll write to me.

PUBLIC: I will indeed.

BOYLE: Yes, the first year. Maybe the second. I'll—I'll miss you, Gar.

PRIVATE: For God's sake get a grip on yourself.

PUBLIC: Thanks for the book and for—

(*Boyle embraces Public briefly*).

PRIVATE: Stop it! Stop it! Stop it!

But Gareth leaves without the embrace of his father, S. B. O'Donnell, County Councillor, and yet one feels, one knows, that a word would have unlocked affection here. There are minor characters like Master Boyle who, in a Chekhovian manner, reveal their own tragedies as they approach and recede from the main conflict; Madge, the housekeeper, bearing the selfishness of her own family, the loutish Ned, who, in a moment of comradeship, tosses his most valued possession to the emigrant. Referring to Friel's work, Sir Tyrone speaks of 'the humour, compassion and poetry, which pour out of him with the spontaneity of a bird's song'.

In four of his plays—the dramatist refers to them as an 'accidental quartet'—Friel examines the theme of compassion and love. The plays are *Philadelphia, Here I Come!*, *The Loves of Cass Maguire* (1966), *Lovers* (1967) and *Crystal and Fox* (1968). In a broadcast interview he has said that there is a popular concept of love which is partly romantic, partly Christian and partly practical. 'What I've done in these plays is to prowl around this concept and view it from the way one perhaps would look at a piece of sculpture . . . look at it from various different angles. The last of these four plays was *Crystal and Fox* and the view of this concept I got then was a final view, a last view. I had seen this sculpture from all these viewpoints. I don't care to look at it again.'[24] No one is as well aware as the writer when he has exhausted a lode, but I think it is within the bounds of possibility that Brian Friel may turn again to the rich ore of compassion and love.

His latest play, *The Mundy Scheme*, is a satirical comedy set in modern Ireland. First produced at the Olympia Theatre, Dublin on 10 June 1969, it has been presented by the Ulster Theatre Company at the Grove Theatre, Belfast. He does not propose to write another play of what he describes as 'similar here-and-now relevance'. Dramatists, Friel has said, have no solutions. It is not their function to give answers. 'They are not marriage counsellors, nor father confessors, nor politicians, nor economists. What function have they, then? They have this function: they are vitally, persistently, and determinedly concerned with one man's insignificant place in the here-and-now world. They have the function to portray that one man's frustrations and hopes and anguishes and joys and miseries and pleasures with all the precision and accuracy and truth they know; and by so doing help to make a community of individuals.'[25]

6

The Belfast Arts Theatre

In a recent history of the theatre in Ireland[1] we learn that two actor-managers, a Mr Knipe and a Mr Wilmot, were prominent in the playhouses of eighteenth-century Belfast. By happy coincidence, both names are well-known in the life of the Ulster Theatre today; John Knipe, successful producer with the Bangor Company, member of the Arts Council, adviser and helper wherever theatre is to be found, and Hubert Wilmot, founder and governing director of the Belfast Arts Theatre Company.

Hubert and Dorothy Wilmot came to Belfast in the late thirties. In 1944 they helped to form a drama group, the Mask Theatre, with premises in Linenhall Street. Their opening play was Charles Morgan's *The Flashing Stream*, with Harry Towb in the cast. When their rooms were taken over by the U.S. Army in 1945 the group moved to an attic in Upper North Street. In this small theatre, seating about a hundred people, was formed the Arts Theatre Studio. There were to be further 'flittings' around the city centre; in 1950 to Fountain Street Mews, where the Irish novelist Benedict Kiely, who had travelled from Dublin to attend a performance of Claudel's

Meridian, declared the Theatre to be 'a house literally made by the hands of the people who run it;' then in September 1954 Wilmot constructed a theatre in a disused auction room in Little Donegall Street. Here the company opened to an audience of 200 with the Irish première of the Roussin/Mitford comedy *The Little Hut* and a prologue written for the occasion by Jack Loudan.

Seven years later, for another memorable opening night in the company's history, Wilmot chose *Orpheus Descending* by Tennessee Williams. The occasion, on 17 April 1961, was the opening of their new theatre in Botanic Avenue—'the first playhouse,' said the Press 'to be built in Belfast for over fifty years'. The Press also reported that Mr Wilmot in his curtain speech 'spoke warmly of the help the Theatre had received from many sources—from the Council for the Encouragement of Music and the Arts, which had done more for the theatre in the past ten years than was generally realised, from the Belfast Corporation, which had for the first time made a direct grant to the theatre, from the "hard-headed and often maligned business men of Belfast", from many private patrons and from the Pilgrim Trust, . . .'

Those acquainted with the work of the Arts Theatre know that Wilmot did not especially choose plays by Ibsen, Claudel and Williams to lend greater significance to the opening nights of his successive theatre premises. They were no more than three in a remarkable sequence of presentations drawn from world drama, most of it contemporary. So contemporary indeed that many of the Arts Theatre programmes inform the audience that they are about to see the Irish, and in some instances the European, première of the play. The Arts Theatre, largely because of the Director's knowledge of what was happening elsewhere in theatre, his energy and, at times, audacity, brought to Belfast the plays of Bernard, Ionesco, Evrinov, Gazzo, Arthur Miller, Anouilh, Odets, Robert Bolt, Giradoux, Cocteau, Eliot and Greene at a time when these dramatists were no more than names to the majority of play-goers. 'First production outside America of *Darkness at Noon*, the stage adaptation of Arthur Koestler's book, by the Arts Theatre, Belfast, is a really fine job,' said the *Irish Press* on 30 August 1952. 'Hubert Wilmot has achieved something which gives his theatre the greatest boost yet.'

There was not always unanimous approval of the Theatre's selection; from time to time a section of the Press, quite outside critical comment, voiced disapproval of plays by Sartre, O'Neill and Williams. Wilmot has rarely been frustrated in his pursuit of new writing but back in 1954, having completed work on *Close Quarters* by the German writer Somin, he was refused a licence for the production because the author had disappeared into Eastern Europe and his play was held by a functionary with the Gilbertian title of Custodian of Enemy Property.

But perhaps the best-known 'happening' in the Theatre's history occurred when the company took Sartre's *Huis Clos* with Williams's *This Property is Condemned* to Dublin in 1951 —one of many successful Dublin seasons. The Arts had engaged the Peacock Theatre for the run, but hearing of the disastrous fire in the Abbey Theatre, Wilmot wired the Dublin directors offering to cancel the booking if it would be of any assistance to the Abbey. The offer was accepted and with the co-operation of the Abbey Management the Arts Theatre productions were moved to another venue not usually rented to professional companies. The story continues in the accounts of the local critics for it shows in what esteem the Arts Theatre was held in Dublin. 'When they opened at the Royal Irish Academy of Music in Westland Row they were submitted to harassing fire because they dared to put on Jean-Paul Sartre's *Huis Clos*. This reaction seems to me to be not only inhospitable but unintelligent. This is a play and a production which should be seen by anybody who is interested in drama, that opens a window on something more than drawing room comedy or farm kitchen tragedy.'[2] Another report stated: 'They (the company) opened their week on Monday night. Then somebody appears to have discovered that Monsieur Sartre is regarded in certain quarters as a Bad Thing. As a result, the group were asked on Tuesday to remove their posters from the front of the house. After they had pointed out that the only method of showing people that the domestic Georgian façade of the Academy concealed a theatre was by poster, the Governors agreed to leave the posters there, provided that the offending name of Sartre (and of his play) were obliterated . . .' Another Dublin critic, on the same occasion, spun the coin neatly by adding: 'Belfast does not really deserve credit for having such a Theatre; it is Dublin which deserves everlasting obloquy for not having one.'

The Arts Theatre has staged few Irish plays or plays by Irish writers. The notable exceptions are probably the première productions of Donagh MacDonagh's *God's Gentry* (1952) and Joseph Tomelty's *Down the Heather Glen* (1953). The casting list of the Arts Theatre therefore, unlike that, say, of the Group Theatre, has been made up predominantly of 'straight' actors. This has meant that the Theatre's audiences have seen the work of many talented young actors and actresses who have come to Belfast, worked here for a time and moved on, as is their custom, to other playhouses. All this against a background, as it were, of some of our outstanding Ulster actors who have appeared at the Arts through the years—Harry Towb, Doreen Hepburn, Blanaid Irvine, Terence Pim, Arthur Cox, James

Greene, Adrienne McGuill, Marjorie McKee, Maurie Taylor,
Viola McKinstry, Catherine Gibson, Maurice O'Callaghan,
Kathleen Feenan and John C. Burke, who has served the
Theatre not only as actor but as designer and stage director.

In recent years the Arts Theatre has been criticised adversely
for abandoning its earlier policy of presenting drama of the
highest quality on its stage. I should add that Hubert and
Dorothy Wilmot are well aware that it was this policy that
won for the Arts the reputation of being one of the most
exciting theatres in modern Ireland. But recently Wilmot
outlined the present policy, and indeed predicament, of his
Theatre. It is his belief that 'only by presenting *entertainment*
can the living theatre survive the intense competition brought
about by TV and the rapidly-changing pattern of living in the
last few years ... This Theatre receives neither subsidy nor
grant from the Arts Council,[3] Corporation, or any benefac-
tory body. Therefore we cannot afford to risk our existence by
presenting serious plays for a minority audience, who rarely
support the Theatre regularly enough, and in sufficient
numbers, to keep our doors open.'

In coming to this conclusion Wilmot was assisted by a
questionnaire addressed to the Theatre's predominantly
middle-class audiences. In answer to the question 'What play
would you like to see in the future?' 50 per cent voted for
musicals, 25 per cent for comedies, 15 per cent for 'good'
thrillers with the accent on Agatha Christie, and 10 per cent
were for 'strong' drama by such authors as Tennessee Williams,
Arthur Miller, O'Casey, Robert Bolt, etc. In response to the
question 'What plays have you liked best since we opened our
new theatre?' 50 per cent said they enjoyed the musicals more
than the plays, 25 per cent voted for Sam Cree's *Second
Honeymoon* and the remainder were divided between *The*

Importance of Being Earnest and *Witness for the Prosecution.*

Among the musicals so popular with Arts Theatre audiences have been Julian Slade's *Salad Days* and a work based on Percy French's life and lyrics, *The Golden Years*, by Donal Giltinan. Sam Cree, a highly skilful writer of farce (he is reported as saying: 'let others write the "significant" plays so long as I can continue to keep people happy'), contributed *Fanci Free* with music by Elizabeth Quinn. Cree has also given two successful comedies to the Arts in *Second Honeymoon* (1962) and *For Love or Money* (1963).

In 1948 Wilmot had two plays produced,—*The Story of Sandra Deane* and *My Name is Wilde*. His only other piece for the stage since then has been an adaptation of Borchert's radio play *The Man Outside.* At one time he liked to take minor roles in his own productions. Nowadays his appearances before the footlights are limited to the Victorian melodramas staged each Christmas. To Wilmot and his wife, the company's secretary and business manager, a larger theatre has brought greater responsibilities. Between them they manage successfully one of the most attractive small playhouses in Ireland.

Put simply, Hubert Wilmot's opinion, based on a pretty extensive knowledge of the Ulster playgoer, is that he cannot stay in business and cater exclusively, or even largely, for that ten per cent who want good drama. It should be a matter of concern to those who keep on saying that they deserve the theatre they want.

7

The Lyric Players Theatre

'I can only offer to make a very little theatre', said Miss
Horniman, 'and it must be quite simple. You all must do the
rest to make a powerful and prosperous theatre with a high
artistic ideal.'[1] If Mrs Mary O'Malley had to state, in as many
words, *her* offer to modern Irish theatre, I do not think she
would wish to change many or any of those words written to
W. B. Yeats and his friends sixty years ago.

Mary O'Malley learnt her theatre craft with an experimental
group in Dublin. It was during this period that she first
engaged herself in a crusade for Yeatsian drama, which she
considered the Abbey Theatre had been founded to promote
and had since neglected. In 1951, with her husband, P. Pearse
O'Malley, she founded the Lyric Players Theatre to set to
rights this neglect of poetic drama.

Half-a-century earlier the work of the Ulster Literary
Theatre had been strengthened by the almost fortuitous
recruitment of painters and musicians. But the Lyric Players
company from its beginning pursued more than the satisfaction of fine words finely spoken; foundation members included

poets, writers, painters, musicians and singers as well as producers, players and theatre craftsmen.

The first presentations were given in a consulting-room— *At the Hawk's Well* and *The Dreaming of the Bones* by W. B. Yeats, *Lost Light* by Robert Farren and Valentine Iremonger's play on the death of Robert Emmet, *Wrap Up My Green Jacket*. In a broadcast[2] programme on the Theatre's work one of the original members, Frances McShane, said: 'The consulting room at Ulsterville House was our auditorium and the window recess our stage. It was a stage that demanded a strong nerve, iron discipline, and very neat footwork if you hoped to avoid being catapulted into the arms of the audience.'

'*At the Hawk's Well*', says Mary O'Malley, 'was an appropriate first production by the Theatre as it reflected some of the important influences which have guided policy—poetry, dance, music and the visual arts, with Cuchulain, the Hound of Ulster, as the central character. The stage was set and we endeavoured to create a style suitable for dramatic poetry.' But the founders of the Theatre indulged in no illusions about the task ahead of them. The preface to a Theatre publication stated: 'The Lyric Players recognised that some ten years would have to be spent in establishing poetic drama in Belfast ... and each season brought substantial success.'

In the autumn of 1952 Dr and Mrs O'Malley moved to Derryvolgie Avenue. This house had what was variously described as 'a long back room' and 'a stable block at the rear'. Whatever its function had been in this staid Victorian residence it became the Lyric Players' first theatre seating fifty people and with a stage 15 ft by 12 ft. Across that tiny stage, in the first five years, passed the traffic of world drama. Of the thirty-one plays presented, sixteen were Irish, three Greek, seven English and the remaining five American, Russian, Spanish, Italian and Chinese.

Reconstruction in 1956, undertaken largely by the players themselves, added dressing rooms, a lounge and a supper room. This extension permitted a widening in the range of productions and the other activities of the Theatre. A Drama School was opened 'to stimulate creative imagination and aesthetic appreciation, to provide a cultural recreational medium and to cater to the serious student of acting and production'. From the beginning Mary O'Malley saw the Lyric Players Theatre as 'a cultural recreational medium' for patrons as much as for players. 'There were', says John Boyle, an early associate, 'lectures and recitals of poetry, exhibitions of painting and sculpture, and all the activities of scene-painting and costume-making. When the Players moved to Derryvolgie Avenue the pace quickened. The new green room and foyer, opened by Austin Clarke, who has given a lifetime of devotion to poetry and the verse theatre, gave the audience a real sense of being "engaged" in what had become more of a *movement* than a dramatic circle.' And George Mooney, actor and producer, describes a prosaic yet characteristic aspect of the emerging Theatre. 'A feature of the early days was the hospitality. No charge for admission or for supper afterwards in the red-tiled breakfast room. Actors and audience came together after the performance, discussing plays and forming friendships. This fostering of actor-audience association was very necessary in the opinion of the O'Malleys.'

From 1956 onward each season has seen a widening of the Theatre's activities. A Children's Theatre, which developed from the Drama School in 1959, gives an annual production. The *Irish Times* described the presentation of *Alice in Wonderland* as 'one of the most charming and successful theatrical experiments seen in Belfast . . . the members of the cast of seventeen were all aged between 8 and 14. The producer, Erna Kennedy, is thirteen; the players made all their own costumes, the décor, the lighting, the setting, were all the work of the children. Everything went off without a hitch; the youngsters spoke and moved well; they knew full well what they wanted to do, and they did it . . . the Children's Theatre is thought to be unique in Ireland.' A further addition to the group's activities was the founding, in 1963, of an Academy of Music with Daphne Bell as Director.

The first number of a literary magazine, *Threshold*, was published in February, 1957. Edited by Mary O'Malley with John Hewitt as Poetry Editor, recent issues have been given to the care of guest editors. For over ten years *Threshold* has published the writings of poets, short story writers and critics, Irish, European and American, a notable achievement in a country where the life-expectation of the literary magazine is justifiably pessimistic. 'It was hoped,' writes Mary O'Malley, 'that poets and writers might be encouraged to write for the Theatre, but the result has been disappointing. The Theatre has presented the work of promising Irish playwrights but cannot yet claim to have thrown up its own dramatists.'[3] The Lyric Players have, in fact, given the stage premières of several dramatic pieces: *The Falcons in the Snare* by Elizabeth Boyle (1954), *The Bloody Brae* by John Hewitt (1957), *See the Gay Windows* by Norman Harrison (1957), and a Christmas entertainment, *The Wolf in the Wood* by Dorothy Watters (1958).

By 1960 it became evident that the private subsidy which financed the work of the Lyric Players was no longer sufficient.

It was then decided that all theatre activities should be integrated into a non-profit-making charitable trust and this

9

was formally carried out. On May 1st, 1960, it came under the control of seven Trustees: Denis Johnston, playwright and Professor of English; Gabriel Fallon, theatre critic, journalist, and a Director of the Abbey Theatre, Dublin; Deborah Brown, artist, Belfast; John Hewitt, poet and Director of the Art Gallery, Coventry; Terence Flanagan, artist and lecturer in art, Belfast; P. Pearse O'Malley, F.R.C.P., co-founder of the Lyric Players; and the writer. Four Honorary Directors were also appointed with consultative powers: Padraic Colum, a founder of the National Theatre Society that became the Abbey Theatre; John Irvine, poet, Belfast; Thomas Kinsella, poet, Dublin; and Rutherford Mayne.[4]

The present Trustees are Charles Carvill, Colm Kelly, John Hewitt, Patrick Hughes, Roger McHugh, Mary O'Malley and P. Pearse O'Malley, and the Honorary Directors Padraic Colum, Denis Johnston and Thomas Kinsella.

In the Articles of Association of the L.P.T. an obligation of the Trustees is the presentation of 'plays of cultural and educational value from world theatre which shall in each year include one play by William Butler Yeats and in the selection of which special consideration shall be given to the work of Irish poets, writers and dramatists.' The staging of Yeats's work is the prime task and adornment of the Lyric Players and over the seasons they have perfected a complex and formalised technique; formalised, not conventionalised, for the human and irrational element is ever present. 'I find', says Mary O'Malley, 'that even the personality of the player is a factor of importance in the achievement of a satisfactory illusion of *remoteness*, so absolutely essential to plays like *Calvary* or *Resurrection*. An intense, highly emotional actor, no matter how good his professional competence, may not find it possible to subdue his personality to the necessary level of detachment and withdrawal. Even the use of masks will not make any difference, if a personal quality is projected.'[5] One critic, writing of a production of *The Dreaming of the Bones* said: 'There was an almost total absence of what for want of a better phrase I will call "expository emotion". The words were spoken in such a way as to secure Yeats's anticipation of what we now, after Brecht, call the "alienation" effect. The result was not stiff or cold, but by one of those paradoxes which are the caryatides of theatre, most moving.'[6]

Each Yeats play evokes its own colour scheme. *The Dreaming of the Bones*, for example, is mounted in grey, blue and charcoal, *The Player Queen* in orange, yellow and black, *The Only Jealousy of Emer* in green with grey and black, and silver fishing net for the dancers. Where it is possible the stage design is reduced to an abstract panel and in a recent experiment the use of such sets proved highly successful in the presentation of *Purgatory, Calvary, Resurrection, The King of the Great Clock Tower* and *The Death of Cuchulain*. The panels, fitting each to its drama, were designed and painted by Alice Berger Hammerschlag who was scenic adviser to the Theatre until her death in 1969. Other artists who have co-operated with Mary O'Malley in her Yeats productions are choreographer Helen Lewis and scenic artists Deborah Brown and Sam Kirkpatrick. Music has been composed for a number of the Yeats plays by Havelock Nelson and Raymond Warren.

'If we are to restore words to their sovereignty', said Yeats, 'we must make speech even more important than gesture upon the stage.' For a member of the Lyric Players cast melodious and *informed* speaking of the parts is vitally important. (The two attributes do not always go together.) To attain a discipline in speech and in movement continual training is necessary and choreography is employed whether or not there is dancing in the play. In Mary O'Malley's experience 'audience concentration on word and theme can only be held by perfect timing, self control and virtually flawless speech'. Freedom of movement and acting style is partly dictated by the confines of the stage. Happily, it is the style that Mary O'Malley wants to revive, the technique fashioned by the Fays for the original presentation of Yeats's plays. C. E. Montague's vivid description of that style could stand, today, for the work of the Lyric Players in poetic drama:

> They take a fresh clear hold on their craft in its elements . . .
> when one of them has to be thrown up in high relief, the
> rest can fade into the background like mists at a dawn, or
> emit from their eyes an attention that fixes your eyes on the
> central figure more surely than the fiercest limelight that ever
> beat on an actor-manager . . . (they) keep still and white, and
> tragic consequence enfolds them; set on that ground of grave
> and simple exposure, the slightest gesture carries you far in
> divination of what prompts it . . .[7]

The artistic director's concern with audience participation in the telling of these difficult and beautiful plays has been noted. Perhaps it is too much to say that Mary O'Malley has made out of them exoteric theatre, but following the Lyric Players presentation of *The Hourglass* and *The Player Queen* at the 1961 Dublin Theatre Festival one critic, Mairin O'Farrell, commented: 'Yeats never thought of his plays as being entertainment for the masses but the production of these plays confirms one's own belief that when properly done they can have a very wide audience—the grave and beautiful diction of the actors, the brilliance of the décor and the really superb costumes combined to achieve an artistic tour de force.' The Theatre has played at the Dublin Theatre Festival and the Yeats International Summer School, Sligo, on three successive years. A London *Times* correspondent wrote of the 1962 Sligo productions: 'the main burden of presenting the poetic drama of Yeats is left, as usual, to the Lyric Players of Belfast, the only theatre in the world specialising in it and capable of mounting the complete cycle of the Cuchulain plays.' The Theatre took the Hound of Ulster as its badge. The design by Marie and Edna Boyd shows Cuchulain with a raven on his shoulder framed in a harp to symbolise Life, Poetry, Music and the Arts.

Productions of the work of other Irish dramatists include J. M. Synge's *Deirdre* and *Riders to the Sea*, *Lady Spider* by Donagh MacDonagh, *La La Noo* by Jack B. Yeats, *The Moment Next to Nothing* and *The Second Kiss* by Austin Clarke, *The Dreaming Dust* by Denis Johnston, *Apollo in Mourne* by Richard Rowley, *The Enemy Within* by Brian Friel, *Romance of an Idiot* by Criostoir O'Flynn, *Endgame* by Samuel Beckett, Eugene MacCabe's *King of the Castle* and two historical plays—*The Risen People*, James Plunkett's epic on the labour leader, James Larkin, and G. P. Gallivan's *The Stepping Stone*, written around Michael Collins and the Irish Civil War. In 1958 the company gave the first Irish presentation of *The Voice of Shem*, Mary Manning's adaptation of a theme from James Joyce's *Finnegans Wake*. In the same period they produced O'Casey's *Red Roses for Me* and *The Silver Tassie*. The association between the Lyric Players and O'Casey was warm and generous. The first subscription that the Theatre received came from the Irish dramatist. In 1959 he sent a further cheque (kept carefully today in the Theatre's archives) and 'a pagan prayer or two for their brave and fine intentions'. During one of the periods of controversy between Dublin and O'Casey, he withheld rights to his plays from the theatre managements of his native city, but gave permission to the Lyric Players to perform *The Silver Tassie*. As a gesture of thanks and affection the Theatre sent him eighty red roses on his birthday.

Occasionally the Players print the names of those who, in various capacities, have worked in the Theatre; music-makers, stage-managers, designers, wardrobe staff and so on. Among the guest producers have been Ronald Mason, Christopher Fitzsimon, Denis Smyth, Bernard Torney, Hugo McCann, Louis Lentin and Denis Johnston as advisory producer for *The Voice of Shem*. 'In so small a theatre', Ray Rosenfield writes in the *Lyric Theatre Handbook 1951–1968*: 'the most perfunctory of sets would have been tolerated, but Mrs O'Malley gathered round her some of the most notable artists in the North to experiment with scenic design', and amongst her designers Ray Rosenfield mentions Terence Flanagan, Rowel Friers, Gerard Hickey, Raymond Piper and Colin Middleton.

The list of Lyric actors, compiled over twenty years, now runs to two hundred names and more. Impossible to name them all, but exercising a chronicler's privilege I recall with pleasure the playing of Terence Nonweiler, Babs Mooney, Keith Stevens, winner in 1956 of a Radio Eireann award for his performance in the title role of *Peer Gynt*, Joan McCready, Sheelagh Flanagan and Lucy Young, Arthur Brooke and Michael Duffy, Peter Adair as the monk in *The Enemy Within*, Louis Rolston as Joxer, Liam O'Callaghan as Cuchulain and a tremendous Jim Larkin, Sam McCready for many notable performances. For a more detailed survey of this creative activity of players and artists, I would direct the reader to the article by Miss Rosenfield.

On the afternoon of 12 June 1965 Austin Clarke laid the foundation stone of the Lyric Players' new theatre at Ridgeway Street, Belfast. Many of those among that gathering of players, poets, theatre personalities and civic dignitaries felt that the occasion was as much a tribute to the dedication and single-mindedness of Pearse and Mary O'Malley, as marking a momentous day in the story of the Lyric Players. Recalling the laying of stone, Mr Clarke has said '... I did not think that Mrs Mary O'Malley would realise her ambition, despite her hard work for so many years. But she has and I hope that the Verse Theatre will prosper when completed and the roof on. It will be the only one in Ireland, and, as far as I know, the only one in England or Scotland either.'

Six other Irish poets sent their tributes. John Hewitt wrote

For Mary O'Malley and the Lyric Players

I owe much thanks to players everywhere
who've set such circumstance before my mind
that I have shed my momentary care
in rapt occasion of a richer kind:
the mad king and his fool; the broken man
who sees flame make the saint; the peevish pair
who wait beside the tree; the harridan
urging her cracking wheels beyond despair.

With all to thank, I name in gratitude,
and set beside the best, with them aligned,
the little band upon their little stage,
tempered to shew, by that dark woman's mood,
O'Casey's humours, Lorca's sultry rage,
The Theban monarch's terror, gouged and blind.

Today, in their new playhouse overlooking one of the more salubrious stretches of the city's river, the Lyric Players offer us a range and quality of drama fit to match 'O'Casey's humour, Lorca's sultry rage'.

For the past nine years the Ulster Theatre Company has taken drama to towns throughout Northern Ireland. 'While we embark on plays from world theatre', says Harold Goldblatt, the Company's director, 'our main concern is with the Ulster play and playwright. We consider that the characteristics of the Ulster people should be shown on the stage.' Few could quarrel with such a policy, and the U.T.C., with a nucleus of the actors who brought such fame to the early Group Theatre, are well fitted to carry it out. As the Ulster Theatre Company tour under the auspices of the Arts Council of Northern Ireland, they are in as an advantageous position as any company to present new plays to the Ulster public. No doubt the U.T.C., under their experienced and energetic management, will exploit this privilege in the future.

8

The Scene Today

In the preceding chapters I have traced the main, and professional, stem of the theatre in Ulster. It is evident that it could
not have made such growth as it has without the tap root of an
amateur movement. There are numerous active societies
bringing tragedy and comedy on winter nights to country
towns and villages throughout the province, and, on occasion,
adding to their trophies at festivals. Some have managed to
secure the permanency of a playhouse. In 1964 the Circle
Theatre Club, a development of the long-established Belfast
Drama Circle, opened a theatre at New Lodge Road. The
repertoire of the Circle (its members were mostly young
people) was similar to that of the Arts Theatre in its early years,
—largely contemporary American and European plays. The
Circle showed an admirable willingness to let Ulster writers
try out their work on its tiny stage. I have earlier mentioned
the productions of plays by John Hamilton, David McGibbon
and John Boyd and to these should be added Jean Cooper
Foster's adaptation of her radio play *The Renegade* (1966).
Unfortunately, the Circle Theatre Club's premises were
requisitioned during disturbances in the area, but I understand

that the members are in active search for new headquarters.

In March 1963, Joseph Tomelty officially opened the new theatre and premises of the Lurgan Theatre Club. Like the Circle Theatre, the Lurgan Theatre developed from a parent dramatic society, in this case the Brownlow Players, a group with many festival awards to their credit. The company leased space in a disused cinema, and without grants of any kind, but with plenty of enthusiasm and hard work, converted the building to a theatre seating an audience of seventy. The range of the productions seems happily varied, running from O'Casey, Shiels and Priestley to West End thrillers and the comedies of Sam Cree and John McDonnell. The residents and buinessmen of Lurgan and district have given the director, Wolsey Gracey, and his associates encouraging support since the Theatre Club was opened.

Coleraine has had a theatre—the Coleraine Playhouse— since 1949; Portadown has its Gateway Theatre, and in Derry a new group, the 71 Players, attached to the city's Musical and Drama Society, have fitted up a theatre in St Columb's Minor Hall. The Derry Little Theatre seats 102, and according to the local press 'boasts of the most modern theatrical equipment that can be found anywhere'. The enthusiasm and vigour of the amateur movement is evident each year at the Dramatic Festival in the Belfast Opera House, where visiting adjudicators have come to expect acting and producing of a professional standard.

In 1906 the Ulster Literary Theatre, under the auspices of the College's Literary and Scientific Society, gave two productions in the Hall at Queen's College, Belfast, At various periods and in various guises, the students and teachers of Queen's University have contributed much to the story of the theatre in Ulster. In the twenties there were the frolics of the Queen's

Jesters in farce and variety, the members of which, as the Queen's University Dramatic Society, could don the buskin with equal distinction. As with most student communities, theatrical activities wax and wane, but I can recall some excellent presentations by the Q.U.D.S., particularly their production of Giraudoux's *Tiger at the Gates* in its Irish première. An interesting chapter in the Society's history was written in the Hungry Thirties. Under the leadership of Professor H. O. Meredith, the Q.U.D.S. organised a drama group, The Unemployed Workers of Belfast, who staged Marlowe's *The Tragicall History of Dr. Faustus* and the *Philoctetes* of Sophocles; both were produced by Meredith, and the proceeds went to 'supply text-books for the Q.U.B. classes for the unemployed'. In recent years the Department of Extra-Mural Studies, under the guidance and advice of Dr. Louis A. Muinzer, has brought us a wider vista and deeper appreciation of Scandinavian drama. Writing in the magazine of the 1968 Belfast Festival, Dr Muinzer pointed out that to Irish and British audiences Scandinavian drama meant Ibsen and Strindberg. Since then, a number of amateur groups, among them the Q.U.D.S. and the Dublin University Players, have demonstrated that the Northern theatre is not limited to 'a few rather sombre plays by Ibsen and Strindberg, which fail to suggest either the total achievement of Scandinavian tradition or even the varied talent of Ibsen and Strindberg themselves.'

In the first two years of its existence the drama group at the New University of Ulster has presented plays by Shakespeare, Yeats, Eliot, Brecht, Behan, Strindberg and Anouilh. As part of a scheme to encourage drama in local schools and in the community, the Department of English Studies invites children to attend Saturday morning sessions at Coleraine where the young people take part in theatre workshops conducted by lecturers and students. A University Arts Centre and theatre is planned for completion in 1975.

The lack of a modern theatre in Belfast spacious enough to house international drama and ballet has, for a considerable time, been a prolific source of both embarrassment and schemes to solve the problem. But no matter how ingenious the schemes, no matter how influential the names associated with them, all have remained suspended due to lack of money. In 1965, in an effort to find a home for dramatic productions, the Arts Council of Northern Ireland contributed £17,000 towards the conversion of a suburban cinema in Belfast, subsequently named the Grove Theatre. The contract was for five years and the Arts Council guaranteed twelve productions annually at an agreed rental. The building was not to everyone's satisfaction but some notable productions were staged there by visiting as well as local theatre companies. None I think equalled in beauty and delight the appearances of the Irish Ballet. This company has toured under the auspices of the Arts Council, but it is, of course, known and applauded internationally. When Patricia Mulholland and her dancers appeared at a Festival of the English Folk Dance and Song Society, a critic wrote of them: 'the balance and the footwork were quite magical in effect, and while the men seemed to be treading velvet, the girls stepped on air throughout'. Almost a decade later that tribute still stands to these young artists and their gifted founder.

For a number of seasons the Ulster Theatre Company has toured under the auspices of the Arts Council. The Lyric Players Theatre is assisted by a subsidy from the Arts Council which is assessed annually; in 1970 this amounted to £18,000.

When Rutherford Mayne and his friends in the Ulster Literary Theatre appealed for funds to build a playhouse, 'one gentleman sent a subscription of five shillings'. Circumstances affecting the theatre in Ulster have changed much in the intervening sixty years, probably, on balance, for the better. The Empire Theatre has been demolished, the Grand Opera House and the Hippodrome are now ornate picture-houses. On the other hand we have seen the erection of two new, if small, playhouses. The professional theatre progresses much in the manner of Mother Courage's waggon; there is the fitful squeak of protest from the non-theatregoing councillor, the occasional rumble of discontent from the actors, the periodic cry from impoverished managements. As in larger communities, an irreparable, and it seems unavoidable, gap has widened in our theatre activity. 'When I look into the future', Brian Friel has said, 'there is only one firm prediction I can make, and it is this: that the gap between what I will call—for want of a better term—commercial theatre and serious theatre is going to become wider and wider.' The word 'theatre' is so wide in its implications that it becomes blurred at the edges. Sir Tyrone Guthrie acknowledged that it could, at times, mean little more than a place of frivolous entertainment. 'It can be that', he wrote 'and very often is. But it can be far, far more. It can be the means of arousing the most profound reflections, the most vivid passions, the most serene joys.' It is very much in the hands of the Ulster public as to whether this outlet for the human spirit remains open.

In this narrative I've tried to show that more often than is acknowledged, we have had good, sometimes outstanding, playwrights. I am confident that there are young men and women among us today who will write fitting drama for the new theatres, for the skilled actors, and for our delight.

Notes

CHAPTER ONE

[1]Hobson's title may be correct but the official chronology in *Samhain* for November 1908 calls it the Irish National Dramatic Company. The Irish National Theatre Society was formed in 1903.

[2]Letter to the author, 2 July 1965.

[3]Dr Margaret McHenry, *The Ulster Theatre in Ireland*, 1931, 82.

[4]*Enter Robbie John*, written and compiled by David Kennedy, BBC Northern Ireland Region, 25 November 1954.

[5]Forrest Reid, *Private Road*, Faber & Faber, London, 35.

[6]*Ulad*, No. 1, November 1904.

[7]*Ulad*, No. 1, November 1904.

[8]*United Irishman*, 20 July 1901.

[9]*Ulad*, No. 2, February 1905.

CHAPTER TWO

[1]*Ulad*, February 1905.

[2]*Ulad*, February 1905.

[3]Whitford Kane, *Are We all Met?* Elkin Mathews & Marrot, London, 1931, 107.

[4]*Ulad*, February 1905.

[5]'Eighteen Years Work, the Ulster Players', *The Times*, London, 5 December 1922.

[6]*Enter Robbie John*

[7]*Enter Robbie John*.

[8]'Eighteen Years Work', *The Times*, 5 December 1922.

[9]*The Northern Whig*, 5 May 1905 (the article could of course have been written by J. W. Good).

[10]Andrew E. Malone, *The Irish Drama*, Constable, London, 1929, 228.

[11]*Ulad*, May 1905.

[12]Cited by Cul Rathain, *The Propagandist Players*, 'Innis Fail', 1906. Quoted by James D. Johnston, *The Renaissance Theatre in Ulster*, University of North Carolina, 1948.

[13] *Enter Robbie John.*

[14] Ernest A. Boyd, *Ireland's Literary Renaissance*, Maunsel & Co. Ltd., Dublin, 1916, 365.

[15] Robert Hogan and Michael J. O'Neill ed. *Joseph Holloway's Abbey Theatre*, Southern Illinois University Press, 1967.

[16] Rutherford Mayne, *The Drone and other Plays*, Maunsel, Dublin, 1912.

[17] *Are We all Met?*, 109.

[18] McHenry, *Ulster Theatre*, 18.

[19] H. L. Morrow tells me that the ballad was composed by J. Winder Good.

[20] *Sinn Fein*, 2 May 1908.

[21] *Samhain*, November 1908.

[22] *Enter Robbie John.*

[23] *The Drone and other Plays*, Dublin, 1912.

[24] *Are We all Met?*, 107.

[25] *The Nation and the Athenaeum*, 7 July 1923.

[26] Letter in possession of Mr Mayne.

[27] *Are We all Met?*, 111.

[28] *Enter Robbie John.*

[29] See Maurice Bourgeois, *John Millington Synge and the Irish Theatre*, Constable, London, 1913, 146.

[30] *Irish Literature and Drama*, Nelson, London, 1936, 205.

[31] *Lady Gregory's Journals, 1916–30*, Putnam & Co., London, 1946, 102.

[32] *Enter Robbie John.*

[33] *The Spoiled Buddha*, Talbot Press, Dublin, 1919.

[34] Quoted in *The Renaissance Theatre in Ulster*.

[35] *Who Fears to Speak* appeared in the *Dublin Magazine*, Jan.–Mar., 1929.

[36] *Freeman's Journal*, Dublin, 11 December 1917.

[37] *Enter Robbie John.*

[38] Quoted in *The Renaissance Theatre in Ulster*.

[39] *Enter Robbie John.*

[40] *Are We All Met?*, 108.

[41] *The Ulster Theatre*, McHenry, 79

CHAPTER THREE

[1]*Belfast Telegraph*, 20 January 1961.

[2]*Irish Times*, 14 October 1932.

[3]*Irish Independent*, 7 March 1933.

[4]*Irish Press*, 7 March 1933.

[5]*Irish News*, 23 January 1934.

[6]*Irish News*, 16 February 1935.

[7]'The play now called *A Quiet Twelfth* was formerly called *Unrest*, and under that title was awarded a prize by me in a play-competition organised by the Northern Drama League.' See St John Ervine's introduction to *Three Plays by Hugh Quinn*, Constable, London, 1932.

[8]See *Rann*, Summer 1952, Belfast, 18, for George Buchanan's account of the founding of the N.D.L.

CHAPTER FOUR

[1]*A Gathering of Players*, broadcast Northern Ireland Region, BBC, 9 December 1965.

[2]*Northern Whig*, 18 May 1937.

CHAPTER FIVE

[1]A. E. Malone, *The Irish Drama*, Constable, London, 1929, 239.

[2]*The Irish Theatre*, Macmillan, London, 1939, 127.

[3]BBC Northern Ireland Region, 2 December 1948.

[4]*Belfast Telegraph*, 21 March 1951.

[5]*The Arts in Ulster, a symposium*, Harrap, London, 1951, 59.

[6]*Lagan*, Volume 2, No. 1, Belfast, 1946, 54.

[7]*Northern Whig*, Belfast, 16 May 1951.

[8]*Friends and Relations*, Allen and Unwin, London, 1947, 37.

[9]*The Arts in Ulster*, 62.

[10]Alan Denson ed., *Letters from AE*, Abelard-Schuman, London, 279.

[11]*Pelican Guide to English Literature*, Volume 7, 201: Penguin Books, 1963.

[12]*Sunday Independent*, 3 September 1944.

[13]*Standard*, 7 September 1944.

[14]*Irish Times*, 29 August 1944.

[15]*Three Plays by Hugh Quinn*, Constable, London, 1932.

16*A Lock of the General's Hair*, Carter Publications, Belfast, 1953.

17*Highly Efficient*, The Quota Press, Belfast.

18*Belfast Telegraph*, 20 August 1958.

19*Over the Bridge* introduced by Stewart Parker, Gill and Macmillan, 1970.

20*News Letter*, Belfast, 4 June 1963.

21Martin McBirney, BBC Northern Ireland Region, 1 April 1965.

22*Philadelphia, Here I Come!* Brian Friel, Faber & Faber, London, 1965.

23*The Arts in Ulster*, BBC Northern Ireland Region, 17 December 1965.

24BBC Northern Ireland Region, 'Soundings', 2 August 1970.

25'The Theatre of Hope and Despair,' a lecture delivered at the Thomas More Association Symposium, Chicago, reprinted in *Everyman*, Number One, 1968, Servite Priory, Benburb, Co. Tyrone.

CHAPTER SIX

1W. S. Clarke, *The Irish Stage in the Country Towns*, Oxford University Press, 1965.

2*Irish Times*, 3 June 1951.

3In 1962 Hubert Wilmot announced that the Theatre had had such a successful first year in its new premises that it had not been necessary to call on the C.E.M.A. guarantee. 'We are very grateful for the C.E.M.A. guarantee. It is an umbrella which could be very useful, but we are very glad and proud that we did not have to use it.' *Belfast Telegraph*, 18 April 1962.

CHAPTER SEVEN

1Quoted in A. E. Malone, *The Irish Drama*, Constable, London, 1929 98.

2*Lyric Players Theatre*, broadcast Northern Ireland Home Service, BBC, 10 February 1966.

3'Irish Theatre Letter', *Massachusetts Review*, Winter 1964–5, 183.

4*The Massachusetts Review*, 183.

5'The Dream Itself', *Threshold*, No. 19, Belfast, 1965, 59.

6John Jordan, *Hibernia*, November 1961.

7*Dramatic Values*, Methuen, London, 1911, 51–53.

Appendix I

First productions of the Ulster Literary Theatre

TITLE	AUTHOR	THEATRE
1904		
The Reformers	Lewis Purcell	Ulster Minor Hall, Belfast.
Brian of Banba	Bulmer Hobson	Ulster Minor Hall, Belfast.
1905		
The Enthusiast	Lewis Purcell	Clarence Place Hall, Belfast.
Little Cowherd of Slainge	Joseph Campbell	Clarence Place Hall, Belfast.
1906		
Turn of the Road	Rutherford Mayne	Ulster Minor Hall, Belfast.
The Pagan	Lewis Purcell	Ulster Minor Hall, Belfast.
1907		
Suzanne and the Sovereigns	Gerald Macnamara and Lewis Purcell	Exhibition Hall, Belfast.
1908		
Leaders of the People	Robert Harding	Abbey Theatre, Dublin.
The Drone	Rutherford Mayne	Abbey Theatre, Dublin.
1909		
The Mist that Does Be on the Bog	Gerald Macnamara	Abbey Theatre, Dublin.
1910		
The Captain of the Hosts	Rutherford Mayne	Grand Opera House, Belfast.
1911		
Charity	Miss M. F. Scott	Grand Opera House, Belfast.
Red Turf	Rutherford Mayne	Grand Opera House, Belfast.
The Jerry Builders	William Paul	Grand Opera House, Belfast.
1912		
Thompson in Tir-na-nOg	Gerald Macnamara	Grand Opera House, Belfast.

TITLE	AUTHOR	THEATRE
Family Rights	Miss M. F. Scott	Grand Opera House, Belfast.
Sweeping the Country	William Paul	Grand Opera House, Belfast.
1913		
If!	Rutherford Mayne	Grand Opera House, Belfast.
Love and Land	Lynn Doyle	Grand Opera House, Belfast.
1914		
Evening	Rutherford Mayne	Gaiety Theatre, Dublin.
1915		
Snowdrop Jane	Shan F. Bullock	Grand Opera House, Belfast.
The Spoiled Buddha	Helen Waddell	Grand Opera House, Belfast.
1916		
The Old Lady	Bernard Duffy	Grand Opera House, Belfast.
Neil Gallina	Rutherford Mayne	Grand Opera House, Belfast.
The Tumulty Case	William Paul	Grand Opera House, Belfast.
1917		
The Throwbacks	Gerald Macnamara	Grand Opera House, Belfast.
Dark Hour	Robert Christie	Grand Opera House, Belfast.
Industry	Rutherford Mayne	Grand Opera House, Belfast.
The Skipper's Submarine	Charles K. Ayre	Grand Opera House, Belfast.
1918		
The Summons	Leslie Lynd (Lynn Doyle)	Grand Opera House, Belfast.
Away from the Moss	George Morshiel	Grand Opera House, Belfast.
Sincerity	Gerald Macnamara	Gaiety Theatre, Dublin.
1919		
The Lilac Ribbon	Lynn Doyle	Grand Opera House, Belfast.
Felix Reid and Bob	George Morshiel	Grand Opera House, Belfast.
The Lone Man	Charles K. Ayre	Grand Opera House, Belfast.
1920		
The Jew's Fiddle	Abram Rish and R. H. Hayward	Gaiety Theatre, Dublin.
1921		
Loaves and Fishes	Charles K. Ayre	Grand Opera House, Belfast.
1922		
The Turncoats	Lynn Doyle	The Playhouse, Liverpool.

TITLE	AUTHOR	THEATRE
1923		
Fee, Faw, Fum	Gerald Macnamara	Grand Opera House, Belfast.
The Phantoms	Rutherford Mayne	Gaiety Theatre, Dublin.
1924		
The Land of the Strangers	Dolly Don Byrne	Gaiety Theatre, Dublin.
The Ship	St John Ervine	Gaiety Theatre, Dublin.
Huge Love	R. H. Hayward	Gaiety Theatre, Dublin.
1925		
Missing Links	Charles K. Ayre	Gaiety Theatre, Dublin.
1928		
No Surrender	Gerald Macnamara	Grand Opera House, Belfast.
Passed Unanimously	N. F. Webb	Grand Opera House, Belfast.
1929		
Who Fears to Speak	Gerald Macnamara	Grand Opera House, Belfast.
1931		
Cobbers Go Halves	Lewis Purcell	Grand Opera House, Belfast.
1934		
A Majority of One	William Liddell	Grand Opera House, Belfast.
The Schemer	Thomas Kelly	Grand Opera House, Belfast.
Thompson on Terra Firma	Gerald Macnamara	Grand Opera House, Belfast.

Appendix II

A list of plays first presented by the Ulster Group Theatre
(1941–60)

TITLE	AUTHOR	THEATRE
1941		
Story for Today	Jack Loudan	Ulster Group Theatre.
1942		
The Heritage	John K. Montgomery	Ulster Group Theatre
Idolatry at Inishargie	Joseph Tomelty	Ulster Group Theatre.
Highly Efficient	Patricia O'Connor	Ulster Group Theatre.
1943		
Legacy of Delight	Hugh Quinn	Ulster Group Theatre.
Poor Errand	Joseph Tomelty	Ulster Group Theatre.
Right Again, Barnum	Joseph Tomelty	Ulster Group Theatre.
1944		
The Old Broom	George Shiels	Ulster Group Theatre.
Voice Out of Rama	Patricia O'Connor	Ulster Group Theatre.
1945		
Henry Joy McCracken	Jack Loudan	Ulster Group Theatre.
Select Vestry	Patricia O'Connor	Ulster Group Theatre.
1946		
The Curse of the Lone Tree	M. Eamon Dubhagan	Ulster Group Theatre.
Borderwine	George Shiels	Ulster Group Theatre.
1948		
The House that Jack Built	Cecil S. Cree	Ulster Group Theatre.
Stars in Brickfield Street	John Coulter	Ulster Group Theatre.

TITLE	AUTHOR	THEATRE
Mountain Post	George Shiels	Ulster Group Theatre.

1949

Bannister's Café	Harry S. Gibson	Ulster Group Theatre.
Master Adams	Patricia O'Connor	Ulster Group Theatre.
All Souls' Night	Joseph Tomelty	Ulster Group Theatre.
Title for Buxey	Cecil S. Cree	Ulster Group Theatre.

1950

The Square Peg	Harry S. Gibson	Ulster Group Theatre

1951

What's Bred in the Bone	Ruddick Millar	Ulster Group Theatre.
Fiddler's Folly	Lynn Doyle	Ulster Group Theatre.
Signs and Wonders	Janet McNeill	Ulster Group Theatre.
Arty	J. R. Mageean/ R. Millar	Ulster Group Theatre.

1952

My Brother Tom	St John Ervine	Ulster Group Theatre.
The House of Mallon	Patrick Riddell	Ulster Group Theatre.

1953

Lock of the General's Hair	Jack Loudan	Ulster Group Theatre.
Ballyfarland's Festival	St John Ervine	Ulster Group Theatre.
Dust Under Our Feet	M. J. Murphy	Arts Theatre, London.
Danger, Men Working (new version)	J. D. Stewart	Ulster Group Theatre.
The Season's Greetings	Hebe Elsna	Ulster Group Theatre.

1954

Is the Priest at Home?	Joseph Tomelty	Ulster Group Theatre.
April in Assagh	Joseph Tomelty	Grand Opera House, Belfast.
Mrs Martin's Man	John Boyd/ St J. Ervine	Ulster Group Theatre.

1955

That Woman at Rathard	Sam Hanna Bell	Ulster Group Theatre.

TITLE	AUTHOR	THEATRE
The Farmer Wants a Wife	Patricia O'Connor	Ulster Group Theatre.
Martha	St John Ervine	Ulster Group Theatre.
Diana	C. K. Munro	Ulster Group Theatre.

1956

A Saint of Little Consequence	John Crilly	Ulster Group Theatre.
Who Saw Her Die?	Patricia O'Connor	Ulster Group Theatre.
Ill Fares the Land	P. J. McLaughlin	Ulster Group Theatre.

1957

The Mustard Seed	Joan Sadler	Ulster Group Theatre.
Traitors in Our Way	Louis MacNeice	Ulster Group Theatre.

1958

The Bonefire	Gerald McLarnon	Grand Opera House, Belfast.
The Lord of Blarney	Charles Witherspoon	Ulster Group Theatre.

1959

The Sparrows Fall	Patricia O'Connor	Ulster Group Theatre.
The Country Boy	John Murphy	Ulster Group Theatre.

1960

The Randy Dandy	Stewart Love	Ulster Group Theatre.
Men on the Wall	M. J. Murphy	Ulster Group Theatre.

Appendix III

Lyric Players Theatre productions
(1951–71)

Title	*Author*
1951–52	
Lost Light	Robert Farren
At the Hawk's Well	W. B. Yeats
The Kiss	Austin Clarke
1952–53	
Before Breakfast	Eugene O'Neill
Pricely Fortune	from the Chinese
A Swan Song	Anton Tchekhov
Wrap up my Green Jacket	Valentine Iremonger
The Viscount of Blarney	Austin Clarke
The Dreaming of the Bones	W. B. Yeats
Icaro	Lauro de Bosis
Christmas Pot-Pourri	
1953–54	
This Way to the Tomb	Ronald Duncan
Cathleen Ni Houlihan	W. B. Yeats
The Only Jealousy of Emer	W. B. Yeats
The Second Kiss	Austin Clarke
The First Born	Christopher Fry
Blood Wedding	Federico Garcia Lorca
1954–55	
Seadna	Joy Rudd
Othello (Act III Scene III)	William Shakespeare
The Falcons in the Snare	Elizabeth Boyle
Comus	Milton
Calvary	W. B. Yeats
Hamlet (1603)	William Shakespeare

Title	Author
The First Born (Dublin production)	Christopher Fry

1955–56

Sophocles's King Oedipus	W. B. Yeats
The Land of Heart's Desire	W. B. Yeats
The Family Reunion	T. S. Eliot
The Frogs	Aristophanes
King Lear	William Shakespeare
Hippolytus	Euripides

1956–57

Volpone	Ben Jonson
The King's Threshold	W. B. Yeats
La La Noo	Jack B. Yeats
The Dark is Light Enough	Christopher Fry
Antigone	Jean Anouilh
Macbeth	William Shakespeare
The House of Bernarda Alba	Federico Garcia Lorca
The Children of Lir	Joy Rudd

1957–58

The Seagull	Anton Tchekhov
The Bloody Brae	John Hewitt
Purgatory	W. B. Yeats
Deirdre	W. B. Yeats
Under Milk Wood	Dylan Thomas
Peer Gynt	Henrik Ibsen
Medea	Robinson Jeffers
See the Gay Windows	Norman Harrison

1958–59

The Three Sisters	Anton Tchekhov
The Silver Tassie	Seán O'Casey
Julius Caesar	William Shakespeare
The Voice of Shem	Mary Manning
(Themes from James Joyce's *Finnegans Wake*)	
The Land of Heart's Desire	W. B. Yeats

Title	*Author*
Purgatory	W. B. Yeats
The Wolf in the Wood	Dorothy Watters

1959–60

Sophocles' Oedipus at Colonus	W. B. Yeats' version
Before Breakfast	Eugene O'Neill
The Emperor Jones	Eugene O'Neill
Wrap Up My Green Jacket	Valentine Iremonger
Romeo and Juliet	William Shakespeare
Sophocles' Oedipus at Colonus	(Dublin production)
The Death of Cuchulain	W. B. Yeats
The Dybbuk	S. Ansky
The Heart's A Wonder	Adapted by Nuala and Mairin O'Farrell

(a musical version of *The Playboy of the Western World*)

Red Roses for Me	Seán O'Casey

1960–61

Yerma	Federico Garcia Lorca
At the Hawk's Well	W. B. Yeats
On Baile's Strand	W. B. Yeats
The Only Jealousy of Emer	W. B. Yeats
The Death of Cuchulain	W. B. Yeats
Riders to the Sea	J. M. Synge
King Lear	William Shakespeare
Lady Spider	Donagh MacDonagh
Mary Stuart	Friedrich Schiller
The Heart's A Wonder	Nuala and Mairin O'Farrell
Purgatory	W. B. Yeats
The King's Threshold	W. B. Yeats
A Full Moon in March	W. B. Yeats

1961–62

The Kingdom of God	Sierra
Brand	Henrik Ibsen
Thompson in Tir-na-nOg	Gerald Macnamara
Apollo in Mourne	Richard Rowley

Title	Author
The Rising of the Moon	Lady Gregory
The Dreaming Dust	Denis Johnston
Dona Rosita	Lorca
Many Young Men of Twenty	John B. Keane
The Carmelites	Bernanos
The Dreaming of the Bones	W. B. Yeats
The Hour Glass	W. B. Yeats
The Players' Queen	W. B. Yeats
At the Hawk's Well	W. B. Yeats

1962–63

The Moment Next to Nothing	Austin Clarke
A Man for All Seasons	Robert Bolt
Romance of an Idiot	Criostoir O'Flynn
Uncle Vanya	Anton Tchekhov
Deirdre of the Sorrows	J. M. Synge
The Heart's A Wonder	Nuala and Mairin O'Farrell
Many Young Men of Twenty	J. B. Keane
The Risen People	James Plunkett
Riders to the Sea	J. M. Synge
Grace	Adapted from Joyce's *Dubliners*
The Rising of the Moon	Lady Gregory
Calvary	W. B. Yeats
Oedipus Rex and *Oedipus at Colonus*	W. B. Yeats
Purgatory	W. B. Yeats
The King's Threshold	W. B. Yeats
On Baile's Strand	W. B. Yeats

1963–64

The Enemy Within	Brian Friel
The House of Bernarda Alba	Lorca
End Game	Samuel Beckett
The Stepping Stone	G. P. Gallivan
Jacques	Ionesco
The Future is in Eggs	Ionesco
Martine	J. J. Bernard

Title	Author
Richard III	William Shakespeare
Next Time I'll Sing to You	James Saunders
The Unicorn and the Stars	
The Cat and the Moon	
The Herne's Egg	W. B. Yeats
The Resurrection	

1964–65

The Possessed	Albert Camus
The Blind Mice	Brian Friel
The Rough and Ready Lot	Alun Owen
The Beggar's Opera	John Gay
The Cherry Orchard	Anton Tchekhov
Long Day's Journey into Night	Eugene O'Neill
The Pot of Broth	
Words upon the Window Pane	
The Green Helmet	W. B. Yeats
The Death of Cuchulain	
The Subject was Roses	Frank D. Gilroy
The Only Jealousy of Emer	
The Death of Cuchulain	
The Dreaming of the Bones	
The King of the Great Clock Tower	W. B. Yeats
Purgatory	
Calvary	
The Resurrection	

1965–66

The Heart's A Wonder	Mairin and Nuala O'Farrell
Ghosts	Henrik Ibsen
Juno and the Paycock	Seán O'Casey
The Fantasticks	Jones and Schmidt
A Month in the Country	Turgenev
King of the Castle	Eugene McCabe
Caligula	Albert Camus
The Plough and the Stars	Seán O'Casey
The Duchess of Malfi	John Webster

Title	Author
The Shadowy Waters	W. B. Yeats
The Countess Cathleen	W. B. Yeats
The Dreaming of the Bones	W. B. Yeats

1966–67

The Field	John B. Keane
Heartbreak House	G. B. Shaw
Lower Depths	Maxim Gorki
Who's Afraid of Virginia Woolf?	Edward Albee
The Shaughraun	Dion Boucicaul
The Plough and the Stars	Seán O'Casey
Anna Kleiber	Alfonso Sastre
That Woman at Rathard	Sam Hanna Bell
The Caucasian Chalk Circle	Berthold Brecht
The Green Desert	Patrick Hughes
Them	Thomas Coffey
Richard III	William Shakespeare
Deirdre	W. B. Yeats
A Full Moon in March	W. B. Yeats
The Words upon the Window Pane	W. B. Yeats

1967–68

Smock Alley	Mairin Charlton
The Shadow of a Gunman	Seán O'Casey
The Chair	Michael Judge
Breakdown	Eugene McCabe
All Souls' Night	Joseph Tomelty
Juno and the Paycock	Seán O'Casey
Nathan the Wise	Lessing
The Wild Duck	Henrik Ibsen
The Plough and the Stars	Seán O'Casey
The Last Eleven	Jack White
The Promise	Alexsei Arbuzov
Henry IV	Pirandello
Smock Alley	arranged by Mairin Charlton

Title	Author
The Dreaming of the Bones	
Oedipus at Colonus	
The King of the Great Clock Tower	W. B. Yeats
Purgatory	
Calvary	
The Resurrection	

1968–69

The Cuchulain Cycle	W. B. Yeats
The Seagull	Anton Tchekhov
Tarry Flynn	Patrick Kavanagh
A Penny for a Song	John Whiting
The Royal Hunt of the Sun	Peter Shaffer
The Quare Fellow	Brendan Behan
Smock Alley	Mairin Charlton
Pictures in the Hallway	Seán O'Casey
The School for Scandal	R. B. Sheridan
The Prime of Miss Jean Brodie	Adapted by J. P. Allen from Muriel Spark's novel
Sive	John B. Keane
Black Comedy	Peter Shaffer
The Cudgelled Cuckold	Alejandro Casona

1969–70

Juno and the Paycock	Seán O'Casey
The Field	John B. Keane
The Alchemist	Ben Jonson
Luther	John Osborne
Phaedra	Racine
Candida	G. B. Shaw
She Stoops to Conquer	Oliver Goldsmith
The Plough and the Stars	Seán O'Casey
The Magistrate	Pinero
The Dreaming of the Bones	W. B. Yeats
Purgatory	W. B. Yeats
Calvary	W. B. Yeats
The Resurrection	W. B. Yeats

Title	*Author*
Over the Bridge	Sam Thompson
Much Ado about Nothing	William Shakespeare
Lovers	Brian Friel
The Passing Day	George Shiels

1970–71

The Passing Day	George Shiels
The Shadow of a Gunman	Seán O'Casey
The Chair	Michael Judge
Rosencrantz and Guildenstern are Dead	Tom Stoppard
The Becauseway	Wesley Burrowes
Peer Gynt	Henrik Ibsen
Death of a Salesman	Arthur Miller
The Rivals	R. B. Sheridan
The Heart's a Wonder	Mairin and Nuala O'Farrell
The Dance of Death	Strindberg
The Flats	John Boyd
Richard III	William Shakespeare
The Silver Tassie	Seán O'Casey
The Flats (revival)	John Boyd
The Words upon the Window Pane	W. B. Yeats
The King's Threshold	W. B. Yeats

E2